After the Bridge Was Crossed

After the Bridge Was Crossed

A Journey of Thought

Darryl K. Cooke

iUniverse, Inc.
Bloomington

After the Bridge Was Crossed
A Journey of Thought

iUniverse books may be ordered through booksellers or by contacting:

iUniverse
1663 Liberty Drive
Bloomington, IN 47403
www.iuniverse.com
1-800-Authors (1-800-288-4677)

ISBN: 978-1-4759-0607-3 (sc)
ISBN: 978-1-4759-0609-7 (hc)
ISBN: 978-1-4759-0608-0 (e)

Printed in the United States of America

iUniverse rev. date: 04/03/2012

Contents

About the Author

After the Bridge Was Crossed: A Journey of Thought encourages people to expand their thoughts, remove self-imposed barriers, and bring forth the inner leader that resides in all of us. Author Darryl Cooke tells us that as a child, time and time again, he heard the phrase, "We'll cross that bridge once we get to it." Regardless of the circumstances-whether there were concerns about getting from point A to point B, being able to put food on the table, or worrying about how the rent was going to be paid-his grandmother's response was always the same: "We'll cross that bridge once we get to it." In life you will never get ahead if you don't plan ahead. When proper preparation is united with perseverance, fortitude, and determination, the combination can propel you to design a strategic plan around the business of your life. Mental preparation is just as important as action; if you don't know what your going to do once you get to the bridge, then how can you know what to do once you cross it? In After the Bridge Was Crossed Author Darryl Cooke uses his personal life experiences to demonstrate that goals can be attained with thought and planning. We must all strive to be more today than we were yesterday.

Acknowledgments

All praises due to the Most High. No matter what name you address Him by; to Him be all the glory.

I would like to thank my parents, Darryl K. Cooke Sr. and Norine O. Joyner (no no) for giving me life and sustaining me in my time of infancy. My covenant teaches me that one should honor thy mother and father so that thy days upon the earth's green land shall be longer. To my brother and sisters, Vasanta, Takiya, Lashimar, Kizza, and Demetrius; I love you all deeply. I promise to keep trail blazing, burning all debris that lie in my path, therefore making it easier for you to recognize it when its your turn to walk.

To my children Essence, Diamonte, Shereena, you guys are my world. I thought of you'll everyday when I was incarcerated, praying for the day that I could hold you, love you, and teach you. With just one thought of you all, I was able to summon the strength to, not only serve my sentence, but complete this book as well. I hope that I make y'all proud.

To Michelle, my other half; thanks for being my backbone. Thanks for supporting me and giving me the creative space needed in order to make my impression on the world. I thank you and Travon for always having my best interest at heart, thanks for being the love of my life.

To my grandmothers, Maggie M. Peterson and Billie P. Cooke, you will continue to forever live. All of the knowledge that you have given me throughout my life is, in some form or fashion, embedded within these pages.

Auntie Roslon, cousin Tarita, Charisse and Fred; thanks for making sure that I saw my children while I was incarcerated. I'm not quite sure that it would've happened any other way. I love you all for that.

To my brother Charles Sanders, I wanted to let you know that I appreciated the letters, the wisdom, and the finances you sent me during my time of bondage. You are the message you bring. Semper Fidelis Marine! Let's go!

To Donamechi Davis; three words my brother I AM LOYAL, la la. Chuck (ES) It was all a dream. Etienne excellent artwork on this book my dude, it was written. We here. Myron, Thanks for the motivation, I love you lil' bro!! 95th

To Raegan and momma Bricks! Thank you for believing in me when no one else did. Thank you Raegan, (*C.E.O. and founder of Chrysalis Community Center*) for opening up your house and heart to me, but most importantly for employing me; making it possible for me to feed my newborn. I literally can't pay you back for that. All I can say is that **Chrysalis Community Center** will always be in my heart and I'm there for you and momma Bricks at the drop of a dime. I love you both.

Diandre and Deidre, I told y'all that I'd never forget again, now tell em' runteldat! To Kenneth Bryant (kg) I love you cousin and I will always move with the soul of, your mom, my auntie Chandra within me, believe that.

Cousins Chris and Keith, I love you both and y'all know that I'll be calling later to bounce some ideas off of y'all. You two are like my personal consultants, I feel like I owe you all some money every time I call. Love family, now that's how you let the beat build. Uncle Anthony thanks for being a strong role model for me.

I love everybody and trust, me, no one is forgotten. Lamont, did we or did we not call this beloved, your turn now. Tippi, Day Day, lil Nikki, Harold, Kay k, boy boy, john john, na na. To all my aunties, uncles, nieces and nephews, I love you all. To all my incarcerated brothers and sisters; keep them heads up beloved, I got y'all.

To all of my young men and women that I speak to at high schools in the Chicago land area. To all of the forums, churches, and boys and girls clubs that have opened their doors to me, I thank you truly. This is dedicated to that whole village that raised me, I promise not to let y'all down.

Introduction

After The Bridge Was Crossed is what I like to refer to as my symbolic journey through life. As a child I would hear this phrase "we'll cross that bridge once we get to it" over and over. My grandmother use to utilize it all the time, no matter what I asked her whether it was, "what are we going to eat tomorrow" or "how are we going to pay for the bills" she would respond the same way each time, "we'll cross that bring once we get to it." It was her way of saying that I don't know and I'm not going to let it stress me out either. She would add, God takes care birds doesn't He? He shelters them and feeds them on a daily basis and He will surely make a way for us as well.

This is how I, along with most people that I know learned how to improvise, adapt, and overcome; from grandma. I needed all of her lessons in order for me to become the person I am, conversely, my grandmother all ways taught us think and continuously seek knowledge. So it hit me one day, If we don't know what we're going to do once we get to the bridge, then we certainly don't know what we're going to do once we cross it. Hence the title After The Bridge Was Crossed.

Unfortunately, I didn't learn that lesson until after I was incarcerated. I was left with two choices, I could either allow jail to define me, or I could use it as a bridge, navigating me to greener pastures. From that moment, there hasn't been a move that I have made that wasn't calculated. This book represents that journey, from the streets of Chicago to the United

States Marine Corps, from inmate to Motivational Speaker. Our journeys might be different, but the drive, determination, and tenacity that it takes to overcome then are universal.

I challenge you to let this book serve as a bridge in your life. It is through economics and education that we will reclaim our communities. We will also tackle issues ranging from abortion to the art of thinking. We will ask ourselves the hard questions and come up with sound resolutions. There comes a time in a person's life where they must unlearn themselves, in order to grow. Prejudgment, only becomes prejudice when after being inflicted with the truth of sunshine, one still chooses the dark. Each individual is a priest for his or her self; upright, independent, and fearless.

So let's walk these walks together, setting examples for our youth along the way. Plan to the fullest, place your feet on solid ground, and continue to press forward. You will be amazed at what awaits you after the bridge is crossed. The man that believes that he will cross it and the one who believes that he won't are both right the question is which one are YOU!

With every eloquent word that you speak you pay tribute to your education.

—Darryl K. Cooke

Chapter 1

The Art of Thinking

When a man and a woman mate and semen is ejaculated into her body, millions and millions of sperm reproductive cells race at a frantic pace toward the female ovaries. Life and death are literally on the line; before you were in your nineties, on your deathbed, surrounded by three generations of love that you helped to create, way before that point in life where you thought, *its either now or never.* Way before you had the opportunity to risk life and limb within the military services, long before you had the chance to succeed or fail at anything. Way before the trials and tribulations of life had a chance to run their courses, you were engaged in the most critical battle of them all, the battle to be produced or not.

Maybe today, you feel like you're battling the aforementioned problems of the world, hard pressed for success, like the mountain is too high to climb, like the hole is too deep to climb out of; like success is virtually impossible. My, my, my… how quick the mind forgets what it never knew… or should I say… never took the time to think about. To the individual whose reading this book now; you're stronger, greater and more determined than you ever knew. You're a survivor in the truest sense of the word. I mean, just think about it, out of a million cells, yours was the only one to make it through the reproductive system. Thus confirming my theory, and making the old proverb true that, "you are one in a million," capable of achieving anything in life. All you have to do is want it as bad as you wanted life; o' so long ago.

The last paragraph represents a spontaneous thought that had just occurred to me, and well, you know they say that the thought is the cause of it all. The words produced by thought have the power to create, save and destroy. Name something in the world that didn't start with a thought. The house that you live in was someone's thought. The car you drive was someone's vision. The clothes you wear, the chair that you have unconscious faith in when you go to sit in it, are all things that started with a thought.

So I ask you, what's your thought? When are you going to remember the potential you possess and bring your thoughts to fruition, manifestation? When are you finally going to have as much faith in yourself as you have in that chair that you're sitting in? You're so sure that it will sustain your weight, that it will support you. But if you ever decided to muster up that same strength, greatness and determination, and applied it to a passion of yours, I guarantee you that you'll be successful. There's no doubt in my mind that you will capture anything that you decide to pursue.

The art of thinking is complex, yet simplistic. See it's like lifting weights; bench pressing to be exact.

1. You have to have a thought; an ambitious drive.
2. You must get mentally prepared and focus on the goal at hand.
3. Prepare yourself for the expected, as well as, the unexpected pitfalls.
4. Make sure that your spotter is ready to assist you just in case you experience it difficult to get the weight off of you.
5. Secure the clamps, then execute.

The thought was to lift the weight on the bar up and down (10x for instance.) Then, the mental preparation was controlling your breathing and getting your mind ready.

Secure the thought in place then, no matter what, as long as your spotter can support you, don't stop until you reach your goal of 10 repetitions.

Even though you had nothing left on rep seven, you dug deep down inside and hit that switch, the switch that all the great ones seem to be able to hit almost automatically. The switch that Ali hit against Foreman, the switch Air Jordan use to hit in the clutch, the switch that a mother hits when she feels as though her child is in danger. You have to hit that switch that allows you to see yourself turning a difficult 8,9,10 into an easy 1,2,3. The art of thinking has the power to do that, and the game of life is played within a 7' perimeter; and that just happens to be where thoughts are born and developed... inside your head. So the point at hand is, that, the man that believes he can and the man that believes he can't are both right... the question is... which person are YOU??

Be aware of the chameleon though, because he possesses the capabilities to forge the appearance of a great thinker, of great thought; but that is not the case. See, the wisdom that's spawned by critical thinking can only be measured and critiqued by who, what, when, where, and how that wisdom is applied and not by your abilities to retain and memorize information, because a parrot can do the same. A chameleon has the shrewdness to interchange his characters when needed. He blends in, and utilizes his handle on the English language to mislead, deceive, and within his mind, in some way lift himself above others.

Don't get me wrong though, because you should never have to dumb down your intellect, and it would be a beautiful thing if his intelligent wordplay was given with the purpose of helping the other man grow, sparking a motivating fuse, or improving his brother man's expansion of thought. More often than not though, it's done merely to display their cynical mirage of superiority. To pat them on the back as if they had once and for all proved and convinced themselves that they now have ascended to an elite coterie of individuals.

You can trust ME when I tell you that every word in this book is used to uplift and expand your thought. Professing great wisdom in this or that, sure they might be highly versed in the rhetoric, they may own the doctor's uniform and they may spend hours upon hours discussing medicinal matters. But when it is actually time to perform heart-to-heart surgery and save another's life, it is here that they remain speechless and motionless. He knew everything in the world but his own ignorance, while the man whom he recited the big words to is on hand, at that very moment, performing the critical transplant.

It was here that we found out that the parrot was not a thinker. It was here that the chameleon was uncloaked and exposed for who he really is, a fraud. But think about how much more useful he would've been to himself and to others if he only had taken the time to actually be who he claimed because, the truth be told, he exerted more energy creating the image and the lie, than he would've used in actually tackling the task at hand. Therefore, the potential had never been in question. He could've easily became who he desired out of life had only he channeled his energy, not towards the explication of things, but towards the application of them. If only he would've used his powers for good instead of evil.

Sure, you could read through this book and be finished with it in a matter of days, but you would get so much more out of it if you forced yourself to apply thought. For every topic that I have given you, stop for a minute and think about it, then find a scenario in your own life to where the passage could've been applied. Nobody knows your life better than you and until you grasp complete control of that you'll forever be searching for the switch that all great thinkers are able to hit at random. So I say to you, apply yourself, fight through all adversity, and I promise you that you'll obtain success monetarily as well as mentally. Never. Ever. No matter what you do, be like the parrot and the chameleon.

Is thinking an art? Well let me say this, when done properly, when all data concerning the matter has been ascertained, when it is founded and based with intellect and understanding, when the crowd's anticipation of the idea or concept has reached it's zenith, then, and only then should the veil be removed and if done with precise timing, what will be revealed is a masterpiece. On the other hand, if you're thinking is rash and sporadic, If your thoughts come and go like the wind, if when the stage is set and you have no idea of when to open and close the curtains then your display will come over as quite tasteless and artless. So I ask you, how could thinking not be considered an art? As a thinker, nothing in life should catch you off-guard. You might not be able to pin-point a scenario down to the precise second it will happen, we're not psychic, I'm definitely not implying that, but just the thought of knowing that anything can occur will put you ahead of the curve.

One day it's going to happen; your son or daughter is going to come to you and ask to go outside to play. Have you prepared your child for that day, have you prepared yourself? From the moment the ultrasound showed that a child was conceived the mind of the young man or woman began to think differently. I recognize the joy that comes over an individual because I've fathered two beautiful children myself. The time goes by so fast and the child is so precious, they're in their infancy stages, unable to think and rationalize for themselves. So it's our job as parents to think and rationalize for them. They don't know what awaits them outside, they have no ideas of the danger to come, and are innocent at heart. They have no idea, but you do?

So a plan should have already been in effect waiting for that day to come about. You can never be too careful with children. I don't care what neighborhood you live in, whether it's the projects on the south side of Chicago or amongst the palm springs of Beverly Hills. The artless painter would just let their child out to roam aimlessly about, but the skillful artist will go out with their child, ingratiate themselves with the parents of the other kids and then set perimeters for the child to play in. "Under no circumstances do you go in the street, and never go pass our neighbors house to the left or the right."

Even more so advised would be if you could stay outside with the child supervising their progress while at the same time building your bond between parent and child. Now all of this sounds simple enough but you'd be surprised how many people are not prepared for this day. So now that we have looked at it in a different light and linked critical thinking to the early childhood development of our own children, I'll ask you again, is thinking an art? A hot head will never make a cool decision. I.e. if your judgment is influenced by anything other than the facts and the truth, you are almost never going to arrive at the best possible solution or remedy. Emotions have the tremendous power of influencing a decision or action. Let's go back to our child that has now made a couple of friends on the block and has made you comfortable with letting them go out and play more frequently.

One day your daughter/son comes in the house crying and screaming with a scraped elbow that is dripping blood. The natural instinct is to ask, "what happened?" Filled with emotions, then frantically, while gasping for breath, your child says (lets say your daughter) that "Johnny" pushed her to the ground. How do you respond? Have you ever given it critical thought? I'm sure that you've thought of it before, but has it been in depth, did you utilize our four steps? Remember, a true thinker should never be caught off-guard with the possibilities of what can happen in life, maybe the exact time, but not the scenario. So as thinkers, let's take advantage of that information, let's work through the scenarios right now together so we'll be prepared when the situation arises.

For the record, let me state the obvious, when it comes to something as devastating as losing a loved one, no one is ever fully prepared, but think of it as a house fire. No we're never 100 percent prepared or ready, but we're as close to it as we can get, because we've already devised an escape route, with sheets pre-tied, knotted and hanging from the bedroom window. There's one in every room, increasing my family' chances of survival. I don't care if you have to stop, drop, and roll or run, jump, and skip... just get there. So again I ask, how do you respond to the situation involving your daughter and Johnny? Let's explore the options; smoke would have been blowing from a non-thinkers horn only because he loves his child more than himself, (which I could never knock because I love mine the same way). A parental, protective, natural instinct sets in and as a result, a maelstrom of love, anger, and sense of responsibility clouds our judgment. From that point who knows what the outcome will be, not even you will be in control because that hot head will never be able to make that sound and cool decision. Isn't wisdom a luxury?

Now, let's do a complete 180 and travel down a whole new route, that's not to insinuate that those same feelings of love, anger, and sense of responsibility are not embodied amongst those traveling on this road, because they are. It's not to say that these people on this path love their children any less because they don't. They love their children just as equally and possess the same emotions when it comes to theirs, the difference is that they're able to hold those emotions in check by first and foremost, creating a thought, working intelligently to logically figure out what happened. Just the thought of you understanding and acknowledging that more than one scenario could've occurred is a self-evident axiom that implies wisdom.

Was Johnny provoked, or peer pressured into pushing your daughter? Was he struck first? Did Johnny sustain any injuries? It's an abundance of missing information that needs to be unfolded before you can come to a rational decision. Do the kids have puppy love? Its not uncommon for there to be some minor altercations when they have no other way of expressing themselves, other than wrestling in the sandbox and calling each other names, who knows? That's exactly my point. **Secondly,** did you get mentally prepared and focus on the goal at hand? What did you hope to achieve by addressing the young boy, Johnny, because if your only purpose was to strike fear in the other child then that makes your logic and reasoning no more even kilt than the children's.

So let's take the other route again and explore other beneficial avenues. As adults we understand that these things happen; it's not the end of the world, so control your breathing, your grammar, and body language. If nothing else is achieved, it'll be a great opportunity to show your child how to respond to awkward, strenuous, or unfamiliar situations, because believe me, she's watching you. So approach this situation with precision, as a doctor would with a heart transplant. **Thirdly,** you need to prepare for likely and unlikely pitfalls or encounters. What if the child is really a bully and literally tunes you out when you asked him where he lived or who his parents were? What if when you reach the scene of the incident, Johnny's parents were already there with smoke blowing from their horns, motivated by a completely different story than the one you might have been told? The situation could easily turn from bad to worse in a matter of seconds, so someone has to step up and be the thinker and the majority of the time it will just have to be you. That's the burden of leadership!

Aggression thrives off of aggression. You literally turn over and give away any advantage you might have had once you agree to fight aggression on his terms and on his home field. Therefore meet that aggression with not passiveness, but with the strength of reason. If done correctly it will completely annihilate and cripple aggression. Fire thrives off of fire, it feeds off of it, and the fire spreads almost at the speed of light, but if you take fire and douse it with water, well, you get point. ***Fourthly***, you need to see the plan all the way to the end; you can exchange numbers with the parent to show your commitment and dedication to order and peace. Each parent can take the initiative to be fair and impartial when it comes to dealing with further issues that might arise with the children in the future. Now, Which ending would you prefer?

Nothing is written in stone but if these steps are followed in everyday life, no matter the circumstance, the chances of it ending on a favorable note are highly enhanced. May I add this, nine times out of ten, no matter how the adults chose to handle our prior situation, the kids probably were outside playing again, as friends, the very next day, if not hours later. So think, think, and think. The situation can't do anything but prove each individual is responsible for himself, singularly as well as collectively. Each one, teach one and remember a lesson learned is a lesson earned.

To think is to produce or form in the mind. To conceive a thought, meditate upon, or determine by reasoning is to apply great thought. Now how much of this do you do on a daily basis? Stop waiting for outside forces to appear, you have everything you need to succeed within yourself. Happiness is not worlds away. It's not a place of leaps and bounds, and it's when and where ever you decide it is. All you have to do is fertilize that seed because it has the potential to grow to immensely.

In my opinion, thinking should be a prescribed class in every grade of school just like mathematics, science, or social studies, because without the application of thought, great success in any of these other courses couldn't be achieved. The art of thinking is a prerequisite, so therefore it makes perfect and sound sense to me that our children be challenged with the art of thinking from day one. Even if the child didn't learn a thing, they would still recognize thinking as an art, and understand that the thought is the cause of it all. I wish I would've had someone pull me to the side as a youngster and stress the power of thought to me, who knows who I could've been had that fuse been sparked at an early age.

The grasping of knowledge can never come to late though. Take me for example; because (figuratively speaking) I have just arrived at a place in my life where I acknowledge thought for who and what she is. Here I am though, in my humblest attempt, trying my best to relay this information to the masses. What's the purpose of knowledge if it's not the good that it brings by giving it to others? I look at my grandfather who played a part in sustaining a roof over my head, but very little was the part he played in my journey of growth. He's a skilled electrician; he's completed numerous tasks around the house, installed ceiling fans etc. He's a good enough mechanic to keep every family member's car running at peak performance. He's skilled in masonry, construction; the whole nine. I remember watching him make alterations to the house or fixing the car and his only comment was, "you kids go somewhere and play before you mess something up." Never once did he pull me to the side and say" pay attention as I change this oil son, because you'll need this later on in life." This was something that I just learned to do as well. Thank God for wisdom

My points are all the same, it's that if we expect our youth to grow and be prosperous then we have to start nurturing them with what's real from day one. From the very beginning we need to season our children with the maxims of truth. Why would you even begin to speak baby talk to a newborn? "Goo-goo" and "ga-ga" is virtually a set back when English, Spanish, etc, is the language that they really need to learn. My grandfather passed me no skills down, therefore his wisdom will die with him and that is quite selfish when it could've easily continued to live through me. Don't make the same mistake with your child or grandchildren. Think about your posterity and the roll that you could play in it, or the setback you bring about by opting to not participate.

It's not good enough that we just send our children to school and leave the growth of their minds in the hands of another. How could you even feel comfortable with that? Sending them to school is not an alternative to you continuing to teach after the last school bell has rang and the flag has been lowered for the day. How could you just willing relinquish your duties as a parent over to another? So make sure that you play a vital part in your child's thinking progress. You'll be happy that you did so for years and years to come. There is no better joy than to sit back and watch your children become successful and productive thinkers in this independent game called life. The joy doubles when you can watch your child pass that same information down to their children, and just to think, all of this started with a thought, symbolic to the growth of a seed. It was planted nurtured and because of natural effects it grew and grew to its full potential, so make sure that your child discovers that potential at an early age.

The art of thinking is a fulltime job, and just like a newborn it demands attention. Attention to detail will take you further than you might know. I surrounded my scenarios mainly around our children, our future, because in my opinion, nothing else is important and I figured if we could trigger the brain on this topic, then the rest would flow quite fluently. If we can see the benefits of the art of thinking as it applies to our children then it should serve as factual that the knowledge of it is vital to your success and happiness. Be shrewd with your thinking, create the thought, get mentally prepared, address all likely and unlikely pitfalls before hand and always, always, always plan to the end!

Chapter 2

My Interpretation of Love

My heart softened with the thought of writing this chapter, because I know (just by being a creature of nature) that love is the chief element that keeps this world of ours spinning in an orderly fashion. Many of people have spent and dedicated their entire lifetime without fully understanding it. Others have spent a lifetime without even trying to understand it. It was once said that love is a symbol of eternity, it wipes out all sense of time, destroying all memory of a beginning and all fear of an end. To take love out of life is to take away its pleasures.

So what is love? Well, I don't think one individual is capable of answering that question for a group of people collectively, but in my humblest attempt, I hope to thoroughly elaborate on what it means to me and if at all possible, let it serve as grounds for debate in you drawing your own conclusions. I often wonder why we do the things that we do and why we're so fashion conscious? Why do we prefer certain cars v/s others? Why, the higher the price, the more it appeals to us? It's these types of questions (here and now) that have forced me to take a good look in the mirror and reexamine myself. So, as I sit here writing, I detach my brain (my mental) from my body (my physical), and sit them directly across from each other, therefore making it easier for me to evaluate myself. Once that was done, it was as if I had successfully blocked out the business of life. The television affected me not, and a ring of the telephone couldn't have snapped me out of my trance. Unconsciously, I had finally done what the elders in my neighborhood had been asking of me for years, to just slow down and remove myself from the fast lane.

Would the rim, shoes, money, etc, mean as much as it does to me now? At that moment, a new world opened up to me and a new train of thought had formed. The self-consciousness that I had so meticulously and neatly folded away in the back of my closet had finally been exposed and confronted by the only man that could do so, **ME**. I felt vindicated. For the first time in my life I had also felt free. Free from the enslavement of materialistic things that I've been brainwashed to believe made me more handsome/beautiful than I already was before I purchased that product. The first step to anybody, and I mean anybody, understanding love is, first loving you! So many people may profess it, the phrase is thrown around so freely and loosely, but very seldom is a format outlined to help you achieve that goal. It's simple in theory, but complicated by the speed of everyday life.

So remember my words, quote them if necessary. Use them as a defense if necessary. The best advice you can get is from yourself. Love the skin you're in and when everybody goes this way, you go that way. When the world speeds up, you slow down. Step outside of yourself and examine the videotape. Understand what the real treasures of life are and within that you will find that love for self. I guess the elders in my neighborhood did mean me well and I've come to learn that they had a genuine love for me. *In youth, I was so eager and ready to change the world, however, in older age I'm that much more inclined to change the youth.*

They say that a wise man should always prepare for his prosperity. So one day the thought had crossed my mind, and I wondered, what if I was on my deathbed and there was no one inside the room but my children and I? What would my last words to them be? As I held their hands scrambling for the words to say, thoughts of our most purest and loving moments raced through my brain.

I remembered making a pallet on the living room floor while my, seven month old, son named Diamonte laid sleeping upon my chest. I dozed off with him and even though I had those small gates placed to block him from leaving the living room, I distinctly remember forcing myself to sleep lightly, prepared for any movement that my son might have made because my love for him would let no harm come his way. I remember feeling proud and saying to myself that I would give my life without hesitation in order to protect his! With those remarks I knew that I was experiencing love on its highest level. Out of everything that the creator could've blessed me with, he thought that highly of me to let me (honor Him) by looking over one of His children.

My son's whole hand had wrapped around my index finger as I thought to myself that this has to be true love; it was there that my interpretation of love was born, true love. True love to me was anything that prevented you from loving what you had previously loved. Material things meant nothing to me anymore.

I remembered picking up my daughter Essence from pre-school and keeping her for the weekend, she was so shy, but so beautiful. She would sit in one spot all day and watch the lion king. I give all of the credit of me writing this book to my children. Having been raised by a single-mom myself, I know all of thoughts that you may have as a child, and I remembered wishing that I could explain to her all that I knew about life. I wanted to let her know that despite the separation of her mother and I, my love for her was genuine. I told her that her birth was one of the happiest days of my life. I wanted her to know that she was conceived out of love and it was there that my interpretation of it was born; material things meant nothing to me anymore. My kids are my world.

Then I had opened my eyes lying there; feeling overwhelmed by the growth of my children. I was overcome by passion, joy and admiration. Tears filled up in the web of my eyes as I held the hand of each of my children and I said to them, "remember that man's life lies all within the present (so shoot for the stars and beyond) the past is gone, (but {to not} remember and grow from it is to forever be a child) the future may never be (though hope is forever our beacon light). Short, therefore, is man's life, and narrow is the corner of the earth wherein he dwells to live, have children and be prosperous. Then maybe… just maybe, one day you'll be just as blessed as me to have your children by your side in your final hours, and that to me was love. So look inside your inner-self, *put this book down for a minute*, and dedicate a few minutes to thought.

Think about how much more of a success you might have been if some one would've just given you true love. Think about all those that gave you that love, but you were not yet ready to receive it. If some of those older people are living, whether a neighbor (Mrs. Duncan), a teacher (Mrs. King) or whatever, why don't you pick up a phone and give them a call. Get the wife and the kids together and stop by their house. Take a picture for them and let them know that regardless of what they might of thought, you were listening; you were listening to every little bit of wisdom that they were trying to give you. As a result of listening to their wise words of wisdom, this is the family that you've been able to create. You have no idea how far your words will go, not only will you touch the heart a loved one, you have let them know that their efforts weren't in vain. You would've taught yourself a valuable lesson, as well as your children.

Your child may never tell you, but once they go outside amongst their peers they will speak everything that you have spoken inside. The wisdom of that loved one will continue to live, and if the loved one's own children were not taking heed to his/her knowledge (after they bear witness to your respect and appreciation for it) you might be the force that redirects their thoughts. The value of the visit will be invaluable, so many realize it after it's to late, like me. I remember who loved me, I remember Mrs. Duncan, the sweetest lady in the world; I couldn't have been any more than 5 or 6 years old in the inner streets of Chicago.

I loved the Duncan's, because they were so unique to me. They were an older couple, 55 or so, but their generosity, hard working skills and southern hospitality shined remarkably. Every morning as I walked to school, if I was on schedule, I could catch Mr. Duncan with his blue-jean jump suit on, (the sweat and grass stains still visible from the 10hr shift yesterday). The railroad engineer jumpsuit was his trademark along with the barrel he pushed faithfully through our neighborhood equipped with a lawnmower, hefty bags, bush trimmers, and rakes. He was a landscape company within himself, who honored those duties to his last days. On the weekends and during the summertime Mr. Duncan would call me over and I was always excited to go because I knew that more than likely I was about to learn something. Once my learning session was over I could always count on Mrs. Duncan to come and give me a big hug and a kiss and then ask me was I hungry.

I don't know if we have those types of people in the village anymore, they had just as much jurisdiction and meaning in my life as my own biological parents. They weren't forced to care for me; there was no monetary gain at all. All I can see is that they had an unbelievable passion and love for the creator and his creations. Love is universal. It gives and expects nothing in return, only that the person receiving it passes it on to someone else. This book is my humble and modest attempt at that, so at dinnertime tonight, let your child know that he/she is loved. The reassurance will carry them further than you can imagine. Get away from the seemingly demands of the world and make your child or anyone else's day. We dedicate so much to our jobs, by working overtime and then sometimes bringing the troubles home.

Today do something different, take off early and try to make it to one of those basketball or softball games that you've been promising your child you'd attend since last year, because when it's over then it's over and we can't get those moments back. How much would it have meant to you to look up in the stands after you've made a bucket just to see your dad standing and clapping for you.

Wouldn't it have made your day to know that you're doing something that was making the people that brought you into this world proud? What about that time you scored a perfect on that test at school and you brought it home? How much would a hug had meant, what would it have meant if mom would've framed it and placed it for all entering the house to see? Consequently, displaying her pride as well, so love your children love your neighbor love yourself, and pour this love in abundance because the flow of a river can't quench it. The downward pursuit of Niagara Falls can't flood it. The beauty of love is to give love. Display your interpretation of love for the whole world to see.

Chapter 3

Education

This is, by far, the most important topic of them all. Education is the source from which great things are achieved. From the day that you're conceived the process starts and as an infant your five senses are put to work. The ability to see all this new matter for the first time, the ability to hear your, soon to be, spoken language. To be able to recognize and become use to sounds such as music, crickets, and the soft and caring words of "I love you" coming from mommy and daddy. The ability to feel a warm and affectionate embrace from them, the ability to smell and taste new food for the very first time is all a learning process and a significant part of education.

The beautiful thing about education is that it is universal and there is no limit to the amount that each individual should or can obtain. Unconsciously, we learn as an infant even before we know what learning is. We have to depend on others to educate us. The progress of my early childhood development depends directly upon the knowledge that my parents were able to obtain throughout their years. The importance of education on all levels can't be stressed enough.

The black man here in the United States knows all to well of the significance and importance of a fair and impartial education. You learn quickly how important it is once it's taken away from you and that's the situation we faced. We were deprived of equal learning in this country for hundreds of years, amongst a maelstrom of other things setting us back severely. The affairs of men took place without us. We were (and still are) considered to some people, to be lower class citizens, incapable of higher learning. We as a people refused to sit back and accept that role. Even Aristotle knew and once said, *"all men by nature desire to know and learn."*

Minority schools are terribly behind the average predominantly white schools and that's a fact. *In the state of Illinois*, according to schooldigger. com there are *667 high schools*. In the *2010-2011* school year reading and math scores were tragic; *there are only four schools with a black population of 50% or more that even rank in the top 500.* **#11 Lindblom, #20 brooks, #176 king, #376 Kenwood. The next ranked school is Morgan Park, all the way at #518.** Every other school that you can think of with a 50% black population falls between #518 and the bottom, #667. And it's not because white kids are smarter nor have an innate genetic cell that others don't possess. It's simply that their resources, by far, exceed others.

I attended a public school that still taught that Christopher Columbus discovered America. I never had a teacher tell me that I could be president, which brings me back to my opening statements, were I stated, that as an infant we learned unconsciously and depended on others for our education. I'm only as healthy as the fruit I eat, so I digested everything my teacher fed me, however she could only give me what the world had given her. Mentally I was held back and indirectly as it may have been, I was taught that my limits might be well short of the sky. To be the president was just a crazy fantasy, far from reality. That's why I'm so proud of our President; for what he's achieved individually, as well as collectively, in this nation.

I'm proud because I can relate intimately with his journey. We'll perhaps, never know how many people Barack Obama inspired with his indoctrination. Generation after generation fought for our right to education. Luckily, we had men and women that wouldn't fold, that wouldn't settle for the title of second class citizens and as a result, in *1954 Brown vs. the board of education* battled the "separate but equal" educational facilities in the Supreme Court and it was a success. The court holds that separate is inherently unequal and schools therefore integrated to comply with federal law. History was on the verge of being rewritten with those five cases.

Before that proceeding, blacks weren't even allowed to attend white schools, to learn what they were learning. It directly shows that they understood the power in education. They knew that if we were exposed to it then their advantage would be loss and the playing field would begin to become leveled. Do you think that so many strides would take place to keep you away from education if it wasn't extremely important? It was something that they knew could mentally free us? Something that could discredit and impugn upon every lie that has been told; their names are wisdom and knowledge. Ultimately, several more schools had to be sued before integration became the law of the land. The door had been opened though, and it took all this, just to be granted the same educational rights. Now who still doesn't think that education is invaluable?

Blood has been shed in order for me to obtain the wisdom and courage to write this book. My mother could only teach me what she was able to learn; now it's my turn to build upon that and give my kids even more. First of all, they will know that to be the President is well within their grasp and the only limits that are set upon them are the ones that are inside of their heads.

The powerful often dictate how the world is ran and those who lack power basically have no say so. As long as you are educated you always possess the power to right any wrong. The old saying, what you don't know won't hurt you, couldn't be further from the truth, because what you don't know **CAN KILL YOU**! If you're roaming earth aimlessly, not searching for wisdom, then mentally you are already dead.

Just look at the road that Malcolm Little was traveling before he accepted that there was still a lot that he didn't know. He also understood that if he wanted to make a change in his life then he needed to unlearn himself and start over. Malcolm X is the personification of resilience to me, and he is without a doubt, the inspiration behind me writing this book. He took the phrase" self taught" to its epitome. *He realized very quickly that the tongue was mightier than the sword and in order to make himself one of the most profound verbal pugilists, he needed to master the weaponry.* He started from the letter "A" and hand copied the dictionary word for word. It proved to be a shrewd move, because from that point on, he had literally guaranteed that there was no word that anyone could use that he wasn't, at the least familiar with. He armed himself with command of the English language, and made it nearly impossible for him to be verbally defeated.

He understood that if you were on trial on foreign land, then American laws wouldn't apply. He knew that he would have to verse himself well with that particular law in order to ensure himself of a fair trial. Within the court, even in medieval times, in order to be taken as serious or even credible, you must understand court rhetoric as well as etiquette. Taking command of the English language was his first step in ensuring himself a fair trial. He went in fighting to make a change in himself and ended up making a change in a nation. Organizations like the United Negro College Fund amongst many others understand the power that is captured when education is seized. They spend endless hours assuring that our young black youth at least have a chance to afford and attend college. They know that the success of our future generations collectively depends on the wisdom and knowledge of those present today.

I wish that every African American understood the severity of what's taking place. By not obtaining knowledge and continuously killing each other off on the street, we continue to dig the slow but deep grave. We must understand that we're hundreds of years behind literally, and one person can't do it alone. It takes a joint effort by all. If we all could just set aside the pressure of saving the world right now and just concentrate on saving our community, our block; what a beautiful thing it would be. Oprah Winfrey's success represents the achievements of blacks and the possibilities of blacks throughout this nation, but at the end of the day, Oprah Winfrey's success represents Oprah Winfrey. I can't let Oprah Winfrey's success fulfill my dreams. I have to make my own mark in this world. If that mentality becomes infectious, then collectively we will get to where we need to be.

Times are getting better though. Things are changing, but we just can't accept or take for granted that it's a positive change. We have to be sure of it; just because we don't have shackles on doesn't mean that we're not enslaved. It's just covertly now. We have black families that are just sending family members to college for the very first time. It has taken some time but I think we're progressing. It is my opinion that we're destine to resume our rightful place in the affairs of men and nations. We were from a land where we were kings and queens, and brought to this land only to be enslaved. We had no rights, we were considered only 3/5 of a man, and we were robbed of our history, our families, our pride, dignity and whatever else you can think of. We were killed, beaten, raped, hosed, spit on and despised just because of our skin. The truth of the matter is that we're not different because of the color of our skin; we're different because whites exploited the color of our skin.

We had no property, no stocks and bonds, no political pull, absolutely nothing. This has never been an equal playing field. We've been behind since forever. *The United States of America Declaration of Independence;* was written by men who had slaves totally contradicting any talks of being equal or fair. To be simply put, the constitution was never written to work in the black man's behalf and that's why it amazes me that *the constitution,* the same one written in **1776** when our people were slaves is the same law that governs the land today. Even with all that against us, we're still here, striving to obtain even more, with the assistance of education.

An education can make life that much more pleasant and interesting to be a part of. The lack of a decent education is the main thing, during any period of time that would hold you back from achieving your goals. The most lucrative jobs in America are reserved for those with higher learning to properly function at that position. That can't take a chance your skills they have to be almost be certain of them. Trust me when I tell you that they did not ascend to the title of C.E.O by mere gut feelings and randomly making decisions. Every move is a calculated step; did not 2pac tell us this? And this is why you need that degree young people. A degree should be mandatory swag attire. This is because it takes years of studying to be well versed in certain occupations. There are criteria's that need to be met, but once you have them the rewards will be in abundance. Never let anyone tell you that a dream is incapable of being achieved.

Oliver Wendell Holmes once said that a child's education should begin at least one hundred years before he was born and I agree. It is imperative to know the road that your forefathers were traveling in order to fully grasp which way you should be going. There is no time gap. There is no generational gap. The truth never changes; if it was true yesterday then it's true today. All life is bond by cords to all other living things. No man lives for him alone. *As Seneca said I am glad to learn, in order that I may teach.* Even if you don't aspire great knowledge for your own use, you still have an obligation to your future posterity. Education is the systematic development and cultivation of the natural powers. By inculcation, you owe the wisdom that you've acquired over the seasons of life to your brother. It costs you nothing, yet the rewards are plentiful.

Experience is the greatest teacher of all, whether by trial and error or observation. Through experience you've become the person that you are, so remember, that knowing is half the battle. Application is next. A man with an education who doesn't use it (positively) is just as bad as or even worse than a man with no education. You can't go anywhere in life without a thorough education, but If you grew up like I did it is simple and plain where you're going without one!

Education doesn't end when the school bell rings at 2:30, there's something to learn all day long, carry that wisdom with you forever.

Chapter 4

Minorities and Economic Endeavors

I had bad credit before I could walk and talk, and sadly enough, it's unfortunate to report that this is not an uncommon practice amongst African Americans and Latinos to be more precise. To state it simple and plain we are extremely uneducated when it comes to matters dealing with financial literacy, and as a result each generation remains in the dark, forced to start from scratch in their pursuit of monetary happiness. We're literally trapped in a maze that features a million ways in, but only one way out. We actually have to go back to the point of entry and unlearn ourselves, getting a thorough understanding of why we chose that labyrinth, acknowledge where our mistakes were made and then correct them. The first mistake was denying and overlooking the power and extreme influence that the mighty dollar has and we've clearly underestimated, (in our arduous, meaningful, and necessary battle with civil rights etc.) the value of economic rights. The pen is mightier than the sword and financial consciousness is that symbolic pen that inevitably decides when and where that sword will do battle, or be utilized. One dictates the pace while those unable to raise there status carries out the command.

Its equivalent to one selling a product and another buying it, not out of necessity, but out of the cloud of smoke, that gives the illusion those material things dictate one's status and place in our society. It's a false assumption that is sadly pushed by the financially shrewd, yet thirsty blood sucking machines within a corporation called marketing and promotions. They're people with degrees in marketing and sales who, are hired specifically to target the financially unconscious consumer that continues to place no value on his dollar. The have honed their crafts, giving them the knowledge to know whether not they have perfect competition or a monopoly. With perfect competition, the market demand and supply determines the price, where as with a monopoly they are extreme price makers. Their mentality is similar to that of a drug dealer. "Yeah I know that it's morally wrong, but the fiends are going to buy and smoke the drug regardless with their last dollar, so they might as well buy it from me." This is the mentality. There are some marketing and sales departments right now, huddled up with a chalkboard, and a film projector with pie charts trying to figure out the best way to obtain your very last cent. And why do you think they target us? It's because they know what you don't know; the value and power of the dollar. They realized that who ever possesses it, ultimately possesses that power. That power subsequently places you in the position to dictate the pace of things in society. They have no problem with keeping you in the maze, because the longer you stay there chasing your tail, then the more powerful they remain and become, therefore solidifying their reign and influence from the top. It's the same reasoning used by European oppressors, Americans, who denied slaves and so called "freed Negroes" the right to equal education.

They knew that with education an eventual insurrection to their rule would come. The demarcation line has shifted slightly (in the political world) from black and white, to a more profitable war over green. Nowadays, you're either on the side of wealth or you're on the side of poverty and whether or not you chose to acknowledge it is completely up to you. Keep in mind that the circus will continue its travel with or without your participation. If that happens, then also be willing to deal with the fact that denial of this new war may also speak to your status in it. The majority of this world is sleep they just have their eyes open. Just take a good look around you, and it will become clearly evident that there is a monopoly in play. Rich people are finding more ways to become richer, while simultaneously and unconsciously assisting the poor in staying poor, it's almost ingenious. For example, I remember when it was all about ethnically and consciously connecting with the roots of your forefathers, for the black man over here in this western civilization. We held up black fist and wore miniature leather facsimiles of the continent of Africa. It was all about the green, black, and red. So we wore crescent moons and stars around our necks, then as things progressed, the mirage of completion overcame us. Before you knew it, we had traded in our black medallions for silver chains, and the new slang for car had become whip, imagine that. Unconsciously, after all that we had to come thru to free ourselves from slavery, we had now willingly traded in the whips and chains of old for new ones.

Stay conscious of the subliminal signs and symbols and you will be able to prevent yourself from being taken advantage of and manipulated. There was no clearer example than with the proper 80's "used jeans" line, which read on the pocket "get used" by Eli Whitney. The crescent and the moon got replaced by the silver (physical and mental) chains, then some years later the value of silver had decreased and then gold was the elite element. Countless amounts of these chains were worn in abundance, and the subliminal and stereotypical perception was that this symbolized success. What a great marketing tool, now it sets the table for the next level of jewelry to take precedence. The next big thing, and that was platinum. Platinum this, and platinum that, which is cool, I rock it myself, but I do it with a conscious mentality of the mental and negative pitfalls that are, or could be attached to them. First it was the silver, then the gold, next platinum. My point is that, if this same type of value were put on the regular average rocks that you step upon on a daily basis, people would then start wearing them at the end of chains, am I wrong? People would kill one another for them, and legal cases would ensue to determine exactly whose side of the property the rocks sat on. It would be total chaos but it would still be two things that remained the same; that the same people who helped to distribute the silver, helped distribute the gold, and also the platinum, which means that the rich stayed rich, while the targeted consumer, most of whom are everyday citizens, who work from paycheck to paycheck, remain poor.

A monopoly is a market for a good or service that has no close substitutes, and in which there is one supplier that is protected from competition by a barrier preventing the entry of new firms.

They utilize every outlet possible to drive home their marketing scheme, newspapers (read by millions every morning) magazines (placed strategically in every grocery isle in America) because, sooner or later you'll have to buy food, right? The television is the biggest and largest tool of them all. The TV networks make millions off of people that want to run certain commercials at specific times, such as the super bowl, heavy weight fights, popular Television shows, and prime-time hours in general. Preferably between 5pm-8pm is when the majority of families will be home together waiting for dinner, and watching a tad bit of television as they try to wind down from their long school and work days. Companions have no problem paying these millions because it has been proven through census that these methods of persuasion actually work, so the chance of them making their money back, plus some, is extremely great. They prey off of our innate cynical and egotistical mentalities, when they sit down and come up with catchy slogans.

These slogans resonate and embed themselves in you like a mole if they're seen and heard enough times, whether you use them or not. They play off of that and they bank on those people who roam around life as a peacock does, excessively narcissist, because they inevitably become the company's number one consumer. Nothing in this world is more influential than word of mouth. It travels at the speed of light, even when you watch an award show; the red carpet interviews have become just as exciting as the actual handing out of the awards. It's marketable because it gives the celebrities and stars a chance to showcase their jewelry, fashion and clothing, where 90% of the time, the jewelry and fashion monsters who sit atop usually give the apparel to the artist for free, just to reel the viewers in and reap the benefits of their gamble. You see it when it comes to sprite, coke, and Pepsi amongst others.

At this point they can even raise the prices more than they anticipated, because the want and need for their product is enormous. Plus, the bourgeoisie will always assist them with making middle/lower class people feel behind in the times if they don't have the latest. The uppity also have been tricked to believe that, the higher the cost then the better the product. They pay the money, with no questions asked, under the presumption that they are giving themselves the best that life has to offer, because they deserve it. It's marketing at it's best to focus on people's inner need to feel as though they've made it, so they give people a way to announce that feeling to the world. Whether it's with gym shoes, cars, liquors, etc! Their knowledge is effective, my rule of thumb is, if you don't own some land, then does it really make sense to spend your money on a land cruiser. If you have not yet established a way to make sure that your future is secured, and then you should really, really change the way you value money.

The educational department in the urban neighborhoods is failing our children and, they have been for years and it is no secret. As I look back now, I think of some of the classes that we were offered in high school and I can't remember half of them, yet, I passed with flying colors. Now, I feel cheated though, because I realize now that those precious class hours could've been spent more wisely. For instance, I feel as though it should be mandatory for teenagers to be taught how to read the stocks in the paper. So many people wouldn't need financial advisers if the value of many were taught at an early age. The pros and cons of credit were never emphasized to me, the importance of it was never preached, but how could it have been when the people in charge of giving it to me, didn't have it themselves. Even when it came to my parents, as I began this chapter, I told you that I had credit before I could walk and talk. The lights were in my name, the phone bill, and all sorts of things.

Consequently, I was a grown man who had the slightest idea of how to read, yet alone invest in the stock market. I had no money invested in my children's college fund. I had no bank account for myself, the value of money was just never stressed, but wisdom forced me to take a more conscious look at the bigger picture.

To put it in the simplest terms, African Americans and Latinos do a sub par job of recycling the black dollar; it was never instilled in us to do so. We were taught from day one to do well in school so that we could get a good job when we're older and that was the extent of it. So we did well in school, obtained the job, and on payday we gave it all back. There were businesses set up ahead of time that depended on people like me; they could see me coming a mile away. It took me several years to realize that becoming rich or utilizing money correctly was a state of mind. I had to stop blaming others for my financial straits, bite the bullet, and admit that I couldn't become successful by being lucky; I had to be prepared. I was working to fulfill my temporary desires and others were working to one day never have to work again, there were some adjustments that needed to be made in my life.

I was literally working for free. But on a grander scale, we as people (black) are the only ones who let others come into our neighborhoods and set up shop. *Then after we give them our business, they take those same finances back and spend them within their own community* where, consequently, we have no business set up. Imagine that. Very seldom do you see Blacks with Asian apparel stores, period. Let alone in an Asian community. Now when it comes to us, (we're so nice) because you can find an Asian owned dry cleaning business, nail shop, or beauty supply with hair extension, phony gold, and Nikes on every block. You can find that in any black hood across the country, and this is no knock to Asians, cause trust me, I respect the hustle; get your paper. This is strictly just to educate my people. Spike lee has been yelling it for years black people, **"WAKE UP"**.

We spend our money so carelessly, with reckless abandonment. *We spend nearly $1.25 for every $1.00 that we make,* and we've yet to understand that not only is college a good thing, but it is estimated that a person with a college degree makes approximately $1,000,000 more than someone with a high school diploma over a lifetime!

Our investment skills have to increase as well, we haven't invested in anything, except the practice of spending money aimlessly, on the latest fashion. Let's start looking at mutual funds, stocks, and bonds, and certificates of deposit (cd's). We have to stop having financial fears, the longer we do nothing, the longer we'll have nothing. There can't be failure when you've learned what mistakes not to make again. Just say to yourself, I may or may not have achieved my goal fully, as of yet. I may not even achieve it next time, but if I don't it won't be because of this mistake.

Also, we need to focus more on becoming home owners, and taking advantage of all the tax benefits available, not to mention the equity. The building process has to start somewhere, so let it be with you, because we unfortunately don't possess the benefit of generational wealth transfer.

So it's time to start focusing in on college funds for our children. The fact that college costs are severely high is another point altogether. Spend less money living in the now and focus in on how we will be living in the future. Children won't die if they don't get that $700 X box. They'll live to see another day and learn an invaluable lesson in the process. They will live without the expensive, overpriced toys, but they'll die and fade into obliteration without a proper education, so spend that $700 on that.

It's ok to get them nice things, but pick your spots and get your monies worth by also using that as a moment to teach your children about finances and the appreciation of it. Give them the tools that they'll need later on in life right now, don't wait, because to wait is to sink deeper into wrong habits. Waiting is a luxury that we can't afford. Instill in your children that not only can they work hard to obtain good jobs, but that they can also own one of the businesses that gives others good jobs. With positive states of mind, come positive results. Make sure that their cup of hope is half full and not half empty.

From this point on, start living your life as a 24hr intern in accounting and you can learn through observation of others. Realize that you don't have to be earning a million dollars in order to become a millionaire. It's not so much about how much you make, as it is how much you save and invest. It's the only way that we can break this cycle. It's the only way to make it out of the maze.

Get rid of all those credit cards, it just doesn't make sense to pay an *18% interest rate* on a credit card when you can just go get a loan from the bank for *7,8,9% interest rate*, come on people, think. We have to start preaching power to our offspring, we're down subscribing to the theory that all the rewards of life, will only be given by the Creator in the aftermath. Our God is a forgiving and merciful God, and surely he meant for us to taste the fruits of our labors on this physical plain of life. As long as we keep him first, and worship no god's but him. Give him no partners, no equals, and all that you obtain in this life is deserved. We need to stop accepting the bottom; it's consciously demoralizing. For example, some of us enjoy the bottom just because it voids us of responsibility, giving them little or no accountability for their actions. Always, always remember that anyone that is successful is probably only one generation removed from poverty, so never forget what that felt like. The school system is failing, so take it upon yourself to educate our youth, teach them reality, teach them to love God, to love one another, and oh yeah, **read the stock market!**

Chapter 5

My Military Experience

It was never a lifetime dream of mine. The urge just came over me suddenly one day. I remember it like it was yesterday. I was still in high school (James H. Bowen on the southeast side of Chicago) and after school everyday my teammates and I from the football team use to walk up to this main street called commercial just to hang out, buy a burger with fries or what have you. Then somebody (I think it was our quarterback named Q) had the bright idea of going into the military recruiting office just for kicks, out of curiosity. We treated it like a tour of an amusement park, it was as if we were toddlers and all of the bright colors, the uniforms, and the novelty of it all enchanted our senses.

Then unconsciously, all the money that they put into targeting the youth paid off. I thought about how I would look in the uniform, and the natural competitiveness to be the best and overcome any obstacle was tapped in to when the Marine crossed the bridge, climbed the rocks, and then raised his sword like He-man. He looked confident and determined and a part of me wanted to see where I ranked amongst the greatest outfit that this country had to offer as well.

Before I knew it we were in the backroom taking a placement test called an (A.S.V.A.B) Armed Services Vocational Aptitude Battery. The recruiters name was Staff Sergeant Betts and I had no idea at that time what type of impact he was about to have on my life. He wasn't, neither did he look like the mental picture I had drew of a Marine in my head. He stood about 6", he wore glasses and he was very calm and relaxed when he spoke. There was no doubt that he embodied and was comprised of everything that a Marine (a defender of this country) should possess. I navigated toward him instantly because I knew there was something there to be learned.

He read me my test scores back and told me that I had passed and went on to ask me what my plans were after high school. I told him that I had received a letter from the Cincinnati Reds to tryout and he said, "well, if you make that then these scores right here won't mean anything at all." He told me that if it didn't happen then I could always come back in to get more details. He didn't force my hand or make me feel obligated to sign up. He gave me room to make my own decisions. After that, Staff Sgt. Betts would attend my baseball games and I would continue to come to the office just to hang out with the Marines. Gaining knowledge from them became more intriguing to me than actually wearing the uniform. That became my new hang out spot. We played chess together and he gave something to me everyday that I could use in the days to come; wisdom.

Well, baseball tryouts came around and I didn't do as well as planned. When I talked to Betts, I felt as though he was sincere when he said, he wished that I had made it. He said that I still wasn't committed to the Marines. He just wanted me to give him a layout of what my plans in life were. We were beginning to extend beyond the conventional recruiter and prospect roles and into the friend amongst friend role.

He became like a mentor to me, giving me his life experiences so that I may judge my own by them. I had plenty of questions about life, but I never had anyone to address them for me in a way that I could fully grasp it. It's also possible that people did try to bestow me with wisdom and knowledge over the years I just wasn't ready to receive yet. Every flower blossoms in due time though.

My senior year in high school was closing rapidly, and I still hadn't made a decision on my future. My mother would cringe at the thought of losing her one and only son to a battlefield. See, my mother was in prison, and she had been feeling the effects of not being able to be around her kids for years. I remember the day that I ran the thought by her; I could feel her disapproval through the phone. It was as if her worst fears were being confirmed. She immediately asked, "who is this guy; trying to send my son to war?" She said that I wasn't signing anything until she met him face to face. When I called Staff Sergeant Betts he said well "I guess we have a road trip then, huh?"

I'll never forget that day Staff Sgt. Betts had his dress "c" uniform on. U.S. Marines have a variety of uniform combinations. This particular uniform was the infamous blue trousers; coupled with the big red stripe on the side indicating that he was a Non-Commissioned Officer (N.C.O.). He had on the black shiny shoes, and the short sleeve shirt displaying his rank of a Staff Sergeant. Our ride was an hour and a half, but my poor direction giving stretched it out to two hours. When we arrived I was filled with excitement on seeing my mom, in general, and also because I was finally doing something that showed my elevation as a growing man. When we were signing in everyone took notice to Staff Sgt. Betts. They addressed him with admiration and respect and it was easy for me to imagine myself in his shoes. He expressed himself eloquently and always remained humble and appreciative of the compliments. Boot camp had, mentally, already started for me. We passed through the shakedown area and waited for my mom to arrive. She came through the same entrance every visit, so I stared at it as I had done for years as a child. When she finally arrived, both of our faces lit up and we embraced tightly, like any mother and son would that have been separately from each other for years.

Excited and filled with joy aren't the best ways to describe my feelings. My mom and I held hands as she introduced me to some of her friends. And as we got to the table the moment had come, Staff Sgt. Betts stood up as I introduced them. They extended and shook hands. They both said, "hello? It's nice to meet you." My mom cut straight through the small talk and said, "so why are you trying to take my only son from me?" She expressed her bitterness toward herself for being incarcerated and missing most of her children's life and she said that if something happened to me that it would kill her. Staff Sgt. Betts took a deep breath and expressed sincerely that he would never know, to the fullest extent, how a mother feels for her child, but he did know that his mother loved him just the same and when he graduated from boot camp, she couldn't have been prouder. He told my mom that although he didn't fully condone war, he did condone the preparation, integrity, and discipline that the military brings to a young man's life. He said that a young teenage boy would be going in the Marines, but that a grown man would be returning.

My mom pressed her fist against her jaw as she drifted in thought. Then he said that whether the country encountered a war or not was out of his hands, but he promised her that he would continue to oversee me throughout my enlistment in the Marines. My mom then looked at me and said "look at my baby, all grown up and stuff." A tear fell as she said, "you know that I'm going to be worried sick about you, are you sure that this is what you want to do?" And I said without hesitation, "yes." Then she gave me the biggest hug and told me that she loved me. She pointed her finger at SSgt. Betts and said, "take care of my son". Betts straightened his two fingers as to salute or tap the brim of a hat and said, "I'm on top of it".

With that the decision was made, and after not performing my best for the baseball Tryouts College didn't appear to be for me. Besides, the physical challenge that the Marines presented, directly took the place of the competitive nature that I received from playing sports. The time had come.

We were driven to a base (a building) somewhere in Des Plaines, IL. Where I and the other recruits were sworn in. We had no idea of what boot camp would have in store for us. The goodbyes to our families were overwhelming. I remember my grandmother giving me a great big ol' hug and saying, "be safe sweetie and remember that you can always come back home if they mistreat you or you don't like it, you hear me?" That made me smile with uncontrollable comfort, but it also confirmed my decision on why I needed to go. I needed to leave out of my comfort zone, become independent, and start a life of my own.

A shuttle bus drove a group of us from Chicago (and surrounding suburbs) to O'Hare airport and before we knew it we were on our way. The females flew east to North Carolina and the males west to sunny California, San Diego to be exact. We were told that when we arrive at LAX airport that there would be another shuttle bus there to pick us up and deliver us to our destination, the base boot camp. We figured that we'd use those last moments to talk amongst each other, get to know one another, and mentally prepare our minds for the unknown that was about to come. We calculated wrong, as soon as we entered the airport the drama commenced.

There were Marines already waiting on us, we hadn't been in California for two minutes yet, and already someone was in our faces giving us commands. Then, as a group of pretty looking females walked by, the Marine commanded us to sit on the floor, Indian style (with our hands on our knees.) We remained looking straight ahead, and I remember one girl said, "Why is that man treating them like that?" Another female said, "Oh that one guy is cute too!" I don't know who she was referring to, but deep in my heart, I'd like to think that it was I. I had to find inspiration wherever I could. Another yelled "oh, I think that they're about to go to the military" then they collectively screamed out "good luck." The Marine responded with, "oh, they'll need a little bit more that ma'am!" We sat in those spots for hours, and as all the people passed us going about their lives, we started to wonder what exactly we had signed up for.

Then, without warning, we heard the command, "get on your feet, get on your feet" and at that moment we knew that it had began.

"Move it, move it, A to B, A to B" were the orders as we recklessly walked at that frantic pace. Single file. All I kept thinking was, "what is A to B"... I found out shortly after. It's as if the drill instructor read my mind, because he got directly in my face, out of everyone there yelling, screaming, and shouting in my ear, "move faster, keep it tighter recruit. When I say A to B, I mean A to B. asshole to belly button." All I could think to myself was, "wow, this is crazy!"

I had no idea of the amount of pressure and expectations that would be placed on me. I was unaware of the amount of integrity and discipline that was about to be instilled within me, and I had no idea that these lessons would last a lifetime. As we left the airport and boarded the bus, my adrenaline increased. The driver said, "now is the time to turn around if you're scared and no one will judge you. You can feel it in your heart if you're not built for this, then just step down." Then he said "it's going to be a long 13 weeks ladies and gentleman. He never stopped talking, so we never had time to think and before we knew it, the military policeman, armed with an m-16 rifle was surveying our vehicle before giving us permission to enter the base. He walked from the front to the back of the bus making eye contact with all those in route. As he exited, the (mp), with the paperwork in his hand gave the go ahead sign by saluting the driver. The slow drive thru the base's interior captivated all of us. As we came to a complete stop, the driver opened the door and from out of no where appeared this massive man, every bit of 6'6 and 285' his shirt looked like it was painted on and he sported a bald head under his drill instructor cover, (a hat that we call the old Smokey). His eyes were a burning red, his muscles were inhumane and he spoke briefly but sternly. He said my name is Sgt. Mitchell and the last four letters of my name spell hell and that's exactly what I intend to give you, when I ask you a question, you respond by saying "sir, yes sir." "You got that?" Collectively, yet unorganized we nervously yelled "sir, yes sir"! He repeated, "you got that" and we yelled more confidently "sir, yes sir!"

He went on to say, "you will do exactly what I say, when I say, look out the window, there are red footprints painted into the ground and you will have twelve seconds to place yourself on a pair. Every individual had better be at attention, eyes forward and I just wasted 3 seconds talking, so you have 6, 5, and 4,3,2,1. Freeze recruit. Don't move. Stand where you are." So when I yell freeze, you say "freeze, recruit freeze." Then he yelled 'freeze" and we all yelled at the top of our lungs "freeze recruit, freeze!" Those who didn't make it were ordered to relax (by the drill instructor) as those who hustled to make it paid the price for his lackluster brothering, nonstop workouts. We did pushups, leg raises, and sit-ups. Mountain climbers, jumping jacks, etc. and we hadn't been on base that long at all. Plus it was nighttime and vision was minimal at best. After that we stared at a wall that had ten basic rules applied to it, one we had to memorize each and every one. After standing at attention for hours our legs became weak and some even fainted and collapsed, it was one of our first physical and mental challenges because we also had to learn the ten rules written on the wall. It seemed as if we had stood there all night. We were drained from the flight, the wait in the airport, and the *"ritual"* on the footsteps. We were hungry and now we were all given some "never dull" (brass cleaner) and ordered to shine every piece of brass in the building; doorknobs, railings, brass running across the bottom of the door, etc. Then, as we turned a corner in the hallway each recruit was ordered to go through a certain door and when we came out on the other side, we were completely bald; except for small patches of hair that the barber apparently didn't see. We all had what's called a drive by.

After laboring for several more hours we were finally allowed to go to chow. We had no marching skills, no unity, no military prestige; we looked like an out of control mob going to chow. Everyone was starving and throughout the course of life, if you never had an appreciation for food, you had it that day. It didn't matter what they were serving we were just thankful and appreciative for what we had. That lesson turned out to be a reoccurring theme; invaluable. Everything was done with a sense of urgency, but yet in a disciplined and controlled manner. We kept our eyes forward and slid our tray down the line. You received what you received, there was no back talk involved, and we referred to it as "one dip, no lip."

I'm not a pure advocate of war, but there's no denying the things that being in the Marines taught me. Even when it came to the haircuts we received, it wasn't all about control and punishment as I assumed in the beginning. Receiving the haircuts was a symbol of unity. It stated that there was no longer this type of person, or etc; we were all Marines! We all had different and unique backgrounds some of us wore braids, some wore long beards, some Mohawks, some curls, but in here; we were all clean cut; we were a unit; who were learning how to set aside our personal beliefs in the midst of trying to achieve the greater goal. If there's any business company out there that is successful, I'm pretty sure that this technique is applied. Not to the point of dressing and looking alike, but to building team work and cohesiveness within the ranks.

They stressed the fact that we were our brothers keepers and that we all were responsible for each other. It was displayed as soon as we got off the bus and some people didn't make it to the footsteps fast enough. They immediately made the individuals that thought they were out of harms way pay the price. This is a cynical world and we all think of self, but that's not the Marine way. The mission isn't complete until very man has crossed the finish line; I'm not secure until my brother is secure. If my brother is having problems with something then so am I! It was a new way of thinking for a lot of us. If someone didn't have any footsteps, then we put them on our back!

Everything came in stages; we had to gain an appreciation level for everything; boots, boot bands, and the right to wear our uniforms properly. We had to earn the right to hold, fire, and remember the serial number of our rifles. They made us take pride in marching, as a unit, in sync. At first when we marched we sounded like an unorganized rowdy mob ready to take action against a politician, but as time went by and we practiced more, slowly but surely it was all in cadence, as if I giant person was marching. It was camaraderie at its highest level. There were men from everywhere, every state; one of my closest buddies named Cooper was from Houston, TX. We became the best of friends; two people from two different places, yet our mentalities were exactly the same when it came to seeking wisdom and knowledge of self.

There were several days that the primary gruel of the day had taken its toll, but I refused to fold. It would be baking hot as we marched on the black tar covered parade deck. Our drill instructor would give his commands; Column left, column right, right shoulder arms with our m-16 rifles that weighed 7.8lbs. Inspection arms, parade rest, every movement had to be precisely mastered to a science. If you were the one to mess up then you would be met by all three drill instructors simultaneously. You would've been called everything under the sun. It wasn't a place for a person with thin skin. You had to learn how to listen for the instruction, while at the same time blocking out the insults.

I remember the first letter I sent home, well everyone remembered, because it was by force. We had three drill instructors and each was mentally stronger than anyone I had ever been around. There physical was one thing, but it was confidence that oozed from them, the redness that surrounded their eyes when they got fired up. It was the strength they displayed in critical situations. We had one White instructor, one Latino, and one Black, but we couldn't tell the difference between the three, they all were Marines, the best the military had to offer. They sounded believable and they gave the impression that they would fight, mentally or physically, until the mission was complete. They were willing to go all the way and their motto was they didn't believe that their opponent was willing to sacrifice the same thing they would to come out victorious. So they told us to "grab a piece of paper and a pencil, write you name at the top", now write, "Dear family, I made it to the Marine Corps base o.k. I'll write again soon." Then they said write "love always" at the bottom. Now fold it up, fill out the envelope and then place the letter inside of it; now give them here. That was it. That's all we could say, but what I really wanted to say was, "help come get me, because these people are crazy." Slowly but surely though, I became less and less dependent and attached to home and more and more dependent on my present endeavors!

I remember one day we were having physical training (pt) where we were, at the least, running three miles and our drill instructor was calling cadence as usual, "left, left, your left right la o'", but today he yelled "Cooke, take ova" without hesitation I screamed "sir, yes sir." So when I stepped out, he took my place and stepped in the platoon and so I started, "left, left, your left right la, o" and when I heard everyone in my platoon repeat it, it sent chills through my body. It shocked me initially because we had never taken the time to write down the cadence or even practice it. I knew the cadence subconsciously only because of the intensity level our drill instructor used when reciting it to us, he just took a chance with me. Then I thought, why me? What did he see in me that led him to think that I could do that because there were so many things that he had to take into consideration? First of all, he had to see potential in me. Secondly, he had to recognize strength and dedication in me, in which, conversely, meant that I gave off those vibes, consciously or not. Thirdly, he had to pick someone that the other men respected; all of these attributes were ones that I didn't see in myself. They were always there, I just never knew how to utilize them, and he helped me discover the best in me. This was my maturation process at work. It made me conscious of my leadership traits and therefore I made every move after that with precision, because I knew that people were watching my every move. I had a platoon of men that sought me for direction and leadership.

We grew daily and some things that our drill instructor had to constantly tell us to do were unnecessary now because we were learning, taking responsibility, and growing as men. When it was time for the rifle range, our drill instructor said, "All those who have fired a weapon before, you stand over here." I thought it was a trick because I couldn't see me telling on myself like that, plus I couldn't understand his reasoning for asking. He said everyone that has fired a weapon before will be the hardest to teach how to properly fire a weapon because you already think that you know what you're doing.

It's comments like that in which sharpened my tools as a thinker, and by the time graduation had approached we had lost about fifteen people. Those who were still there felt worthy of being there. We felt invincible because we knew that if we could make it through this, then we could make it through anything. We had practiced graduation for weeks as our senior drill instructor announced, "platoon 2073 (twenty-seventy three) dismissed" and we would do an about face and then fall back in to formation, this went on for fourteen days. We went back and forth. So on graduation day our pace was frantic, a lot of people's family members came to San Diego. Ca. and as we marched, the feeling of admiration came over me and I felt myself shed the shell of boyhood, as I became a man. Tears of a soldier fell as my senior drill instructor said, "platoon 2073 dismissed" I looked at the man to my right and then the left as we realized that we were officially United States Marines! For the first time our Sr. drill instructor finally told us that he was proud of us.

It was one of the most beautiful feelings of my life. Now that I'm older I'm able to view the military objectively for the good and the bad. For one, as I stated previously, an appreciation level for the little things in life was stressed, because you never knew when a moment could be your last. Also discipline and respect for authority (as well as people in general) was enforced to the fullest. Leadership traits were brought to the forefront and accepted by each individual. Bonds were formed that can't be broken. There is no way that I could be stranded in adversity and not be able to call one of my Marine brothers to assist me; *NO WHERE in this nation!* *UH RAHH!*

Now on a larger scale, I'm forced to think of the fact that I volunteered for something that could have literally cost me my life, with one signature from the President. It would probably be for a war that I personally have no understanding of, yet was willing to die for. At the age of 18 I'm able to go to war and give my life, but I'm unable to go into a store and legally buy a beer. At 18, I was taught how to fire a 9mm and an m-16 rifle, with remarkable accuracy for up to 500 yards, break my weapon down to the firing pin in one minute and put it back together in under two minutes. I was trained how to kill, and its just unfortunate that this same training was held against me during my sentencing. I'm not excusing myself of any wrongful doing; I'm just saying that there's enough blame to go around. Why is the use of your weapon only approved if the government says so? Why does it have to be on their behalf? If attempted murder is wrong, it should be wrong across the board, what's the difference between the two? Countries can be equated to local gangs; they both fight over the power of land, money, and drugs, just on different levels. A homeless veteran that I met once told me that the Marines taught him how to kill but they never taught him how to stop.

All of the commercials were targeted at the young 18 to 22 year old man's ego and pride. The Marine climbing the cliff, the culmination of receiving the uniform and sword upon completion all plays its part. The commercial with the military men flying jets and all types of aircraft is enticing but it isn't disclosed that the only people who fly these vessels are people who have come into the military with, at least, an Associates degree. You would have to be an Officer, and the same goes for the sword. All these things are only accessible to officers, people who elected to go to school first before joining the Marines.

The Marines utilize advertising and target specific age groups just like any other business, but there's no substitute for what I learned. Your travel is minimal, not like you'd think it would be, but you'll be on your own; making your own way. You will do one year overseas on each term. The rest is spent wherever you are stationed. So, if you sign up for the military make sure it's really what you want to do, and if you do go; you might as well get an Associates degree first. It will increase your rank immediately, making you an officer; increasing your other options, as well as your pay.

Chapter 6

The Penal System

Well there I was, the son of an unstable father, the son of an incarcerated mother, yet I managed to fight my way through against the odds. I received good grades, never drank, never did drugs and never had anything more than a jaywalking ticket. I had never seen the inside of the county jail. I had even tried out for the Cincinnati reds during high school. I didn't make it, to say the least, but nevertheless, I graduated on time and I served in the United States Marine Corps. I had two beautiful children, and I was married working as a switchman for Norfolk southern railroad. I was living my dream, but problems arose.

I was only 24, and immaturity, jealousy, and pride had roots deeply planted in me and in one instance; a role model citizen was fighting a domestic violence case. I was found guilty, as I should've been. I shot through a glass door, and either the glass or the bullet grazed my ex wife on the hip, absolutely the worst day of my life. I absolutely hate day. I'm thankful to Allah, though, that no one was seriously hurt. I never imagined myself in such a horrible position; I just got caught up in trying to protect a devilish falsehood called pride.

Nevertheless, I didn't feel as though I deserved twelve years at 85%. That meant that I would have to spend over a decade behind bars, in which

I did. I can just imagine how much time I would've received if I had had any record what so ever, if I wasn't a working class citizen, or a veteran of the U.S.M.C. The minimum was six years, and I felt as though if the minimum criterion was fit for anyone, it should've been me, but that wasn't the case. So as I walked into Menard, one of the most dangerous jails in the country, I remember saying, "Wow, I thought I'd never see the inside of the walls of a maximum security penitentiary." I thought that all the stories about jail were just that, stories. I found out quickly that they were real though.

One gang was here, and the other there, and those that weren't in a gang had to come together as one just to survive. Certain phones were for certain mobs. The whites had the skinheads, amongst other affiliations, and a war could break out at any moment. Every mob had shanks and knives the size of your grandmother's kitchen set. Everything had a format; nothing ran without a system. People were extorted, beat nearly to death, and even raped. When shakedowns came about, (that's when officers check for contraband) we were forced to bend over and subjected to another man (an officer) looking into my asshole checking for contraband. I felt degraded and humiliated; I mean just think about it, you haven't even seen your own asshole before. It's a very uncomfortable situation to say the least.

Before my incarceration though, I was just like everybody else, I had my own problems. I mean, I knew for a fact that most of the police on the street were crooked, and I had only heard word of mouth from my buddies how the court system operated.

For the most part, I believed that the judicial system worked. I knew that a lot of people locked up were innocent, but I never knew the magnitude of the blatant and outright disregard of the law that prosecutors and states attorneys had by intentionally slamming innocent people with ungodly time. I never took the time out to investigate that because I never saw how it did, or could've directly affected me. That was my first mistake. I was too busy occupied with my life, materialism, and the other false-truths of the world. I had to go to work, and as soon as I got home it was time to eat, take a shower and spend time with my kids. Then it was time for work again. I had disconcerted myself with the failures of society. Sad to say, but I was unconscious in those days. I had become complacent and over the years, society, as a whole, has had a pacifier placed in our mouths and we've been rocked to sleep.

Basically, what the government is saying is that we know that you are a microwave nation. We know that you want everything instantaneously, and we know that collectively we are lazy people so they came up with a *panacea,* a solution which basically states that, we will go to work as citizens for at least 40 hrs A week, full-time in order to take care of yourself, your wife, and your children. You'll use that money to buy a house, a car, and all of the other necessities in life. First and foremost we're going to take taxes directly out of your checks to pay the politicians (the people who will make the bad guys of society disappear) we know that you don't want to deal with the outcasts of society yourself, so for a small fee, we'll take care of that for you. Can you see how we've just relinquished our powers and our responsibilities as a society?

It's just as if we've adopted the faith of idol worshippers of other lands. See, back then at the end of every year; every individual would take all of their sins, wrong-doings; join them collectively and place them all upon the head of one certain individual set apart to bear the sins. That individual now becomes the scapegoat for all collectively, and these people (society) actually believed that when they drove them into different lands that they were actually freed from sin and released from further obligation. **The Holy Koran of The Moorish Science Temple of America: Chapter XVI Pilates Final Efforts to Release Jesus Fails He Washes Hands in Feigned Innocence** verse three *"The man becomes a scapegoat for the multitudes; and they believe that when they drive him forth into the wilds, or in to foreign lands, they are released from sins."* Can you not see the fault in this system, in this train of thought?

These are just superstitions professed by one person and believed and followed by the rest. Just think about it for a second, once the individual is exiled and cast out of the land, (your land) all that happens is that the ousted individual settles in a new land where they will just display the same characteristics as they did in your land. Our cynical and narcissistic mentality never even gave thought to how the next land or man would be affected. Conversely, the illness that the exiled possessed, in the first place, had never been addressed. All that happened is that the hierarchy appeased the people of the land by simply transferring the problem to another land (along with their own sins as extra incentive) that they believed was millions of miles away, some place that was unlike theirs.

Now let's bring the issue to modern times. I believe that this issue does set grounds for concern or at least deserves to have some type of thought applied to it. In my opinion, our judicial system, and our penal institutions still reflect the land where the criminals were driven too. It serves as a way for the politician to appease society and quickly rid them of the problem.

Just to have it on record, I don't wish to rid states of prisons, is not my point at all. Jails, although harsh, are very necessary. The truth of the matter is that a lot of people need it. The jail system (the so-called department of corrections) only works if it serves as a rehabilitation source and not as a warehouse, a dismal crypt, a self dug grave. Some might say that the criminal got exactly what they deserved and in some instances, I agree, for the most part. For example if you've raped someone, I believe you're getting exactly what you deserve. Also, to take someone's life, even in self-defense, is terrible, but to randomly, unconsciously, and purposely take another's life causes for a stiff penalty.

The selling of drugs hurts society as a whole, but I say this, if we're going to stand on the law in one direction then it also must be applied in the other. It puzzles me that a catholic priest can fondle a child (which makes him a pedophile) and basically gets away with a slap on the wrist. Now when it comes to these two offenses rape and pedophilia, I'm not so sure that there is a rehabilitation program for that, I could be wrong, that's just my opinion. For the others, society still may say that they also should be caged away 24/7 like an animal at the nearest zoo, but all I ask is that you hear my reasoning out. A couple of years ago I was just like some, I had a lot of faith in the system and it was just hard to believe that a veil had been pulled over my eyes. Once incarcerated, I've come to realize that society has not received an honest and clear understanding of the system, yet it's societies hard-earned dollars that pay the salaries of the staff. That is what's meant when it is said that you (as society) pay to maintain the imprisonment of the convicted. Believe me, when I tell that if you're under the pretense that all of your funds are used to clothe, house, and feed the inmate then you are sadly mistaken and the government owes you a healthy refund.

Also, when it comes to the education of inmates within the penal institution *nothing is free.* Just as incarceration is the price we pay for our crime, our freedom is the price we pay for our education; now who among you are willing to sacrifice that? Why wouldn't I get an education, not to would be asinine? Wouldn't you consider that part of rehabilitation? Further more, the few things that we do learn are only things that our great public school system failed to teach us in high school. To close on this point, while our academic classes are monetarily free, our trade classes are not. For example, if you decide to take construction, culinary arts, or any other concentrated trade then it will assuredly cost you approximately $93 per credit.

The food that we eat is of the lowest grade, if it's graded at all and even if they (the institution) claimed to spend a lot of money in dietary then, it doesn't matter because they make that money back 5x's over at the institutional commissary. It's here that all defected merchandise is sold. Say for instance a 13" television that they sell to us for $120 is valued at $40.00 in society. Now, they can say that the inmate should be happy that he could even have a television. Well yes, we're thankful for them because without it many would probably go crazy. More aggressive actions would ensue, cellmates would become easily agitated, but on the other hand I wish that they would take the television away because it has served to well as a pacifier, it has knocked the fight out of a lot of people.

Innocent men have become complacent and have literally given up their fight for freedom. Even those that are guilty, but didn't deserve the upgraded charges along with the excess time have given up. So I say to society, I agree with you. Take your televisions back so that I can substitute them with G.E.D, college, and law books.

They won't take commissary away though, why not you say, because it generates too much revenue. There are approximately 3500 inmates at every prison and more than half of them will go to commissary weekly and spend an average of $30 dollars. You do the math on that one. So my point is that the commissary serves the needs of the institution more so than it does the needs of the inmate and nobody can convince me otherwise.

It hurts me deeply every time I think about the actions that caused me to become incarcerated, and when I think about the effect that it's had on my children. It's not a day that I don't die slowly. It breaks me down to my knees, and one day since I was already engaged in prayer, I decided to ask God for forgiveness. I never though that it actually worked, but let the truth be told; it wasn't until the point that I was actually able to forgive myself. The heeling process had started and my next step was to call my ex-wife and apologize, whether she would accept it or not did not was out of my hands. I had to do what I had to do in order to free myself. Since that moment, even though I was still incarcerated, I had finally become free and I never turned back. I took everything more serious, the absence of my kids in my arms brought tears to my eyes, and the inspiration for this book was born.

Whether it was the glass or a bullet that caused the harm in my situation is irrelevant at this point, because the fact still remains that I committed a felony. I AGREE WITH THIS STATEMENT WHOLEHEARTEDLY! As a result of my actions, the state sentenced me to 12 years at 85%.

Also, if rehabilitation was the true plan, than I do feel as though they should have sentenced me to mandatory anger management classes. Isn't that what the department of corrections is for? Wasn't it designed to be a place of reform and rehabilitation? This is where I feel as though the system failed you as a society and me as an individual. What if I needed some force outside of myself to help me get my act together? What if I needed intensive professional help? This means that for over a decade I would've sat inside the penal institution idle, wasting valuable time that clearly could've been used for mandatory rehabilitation. Instead, the convict's time was used debating with other inmates on how to make themselves a better criminal.

When you see (recidivism) repeat offenders of crimes such as pedophile and rape, this is one of the reasons why. Treatment is not always mandatory, and with these two particular charges I don't know if the mandatory treatment is enough.

Again, I'm not saying that what I did wasn't wrong, because it was. I wouldn't dare try to justify it, I'm just stating that the correctional system is very inconsistent when it comes to sentencing people for attempt murders, drugs, etc.

Further more, it amazes me that a gang member, local drug dealer and a pedophile can go to jail on the same day, and the pedophile will receive the lightest sentence, and be released first, with absolutely no rehabilitation or reform applied. It's my belief that society is completely unaware of the total significance of this.

Where are your tax dollars going? All that the system did was exile the criminal (warehouse him, stamp him, and brand him with a number). They hold him/her until they're completely cut off from current affairs in society (out of sight, out of mind.) Then, upon that forced outdate the inmate is just released back into society. With that kind of format the ex-offender chances for survival are minimal. His chances of converting back to his old ways are great.

Before I came to prison, had I not had at least a partial understanding between right and wrong, had my family not instilled in me some morals and ethics, I would've only departed jail as a better criminal and worse of a person. Luckily, I was already blessed with the understanding that nothing in life will happen for me unless I make it happen. Fortunately, I had other conscious, self-motivated inmates who guided and walked with me in the right direction, and forced me to keep reading, and learning. Had they not, there's no telling what type of mischief I might have gotten into. *I took the initiative to enroll myself in anger management class,* whether I had a problem or not. I felt that it was an opportunity to learn something, possibly how to help and deal with other people who might be suffering from anger management. It felt good too, if I may add.

For the first time in my life I was taking responsibility for myself, and at the same time thinking about helping others. It felt good to listen to others, because it made me realize that my petty issues weren't so bad at all. I learned humility for the first time and it has been helping me ever since. I was proud of myself and it was in this class that made me realize that I should've been ordered to take the class, because I needed it. This is why I say that the system failed me. I'm lucky that the institution that I was in offered that class because all institutions don't. I was blessed to have seen the big picture, and every time that I received a cellmate that couldn't read his mail, that couldn't write, that couldn't verbally express himself adequately, it made me appreciate the gifts that the creator had bestowed upon me. My purpose for life was changing, and I can't explain to you how compelled I felt to uplift every male that I came across. It was my way of expressing my appreciation to the creator.

I felt as though I was picking up where the judicial system failed, because whether everyone wants to accept it or not, *eight out of ten inmates will be released again one day who could, in turn, be your next door neighbor.* Most people don't want an ex-offender as a neighbor, but where else would you prefer to send them, (us)? There's no where to exile them to, sooner or later we're going to have to take hold of and grasp the idea of better rehabilitation methods.

Most people are capable of rehabilitation. I'm living proof of that; so was Malcolm X, etc. not to put myself anywhere near the category of a Malcolm X, I just wanted to show you the possibilities of man, because in my opinion, he's the paragon of success. The system is flawed from the beginning and it's no secret that it's targeted at the minority, the poor. The public defender is nothing more than a puppet for the state and they will make sure that the county keeps their conviction rate at a certain level, because they will definitely receive more funds for that.

My time has winded down as an inmate in the Illinois department of corrections, my debt to society has been paid in full, but mainly my debt to myself will be paid. We have been convinced to believe that time heels all wounds, but I disagree, because if you don't take the correct steps to recovery, if you don't engage in the correct treatment, then there's nothing that time can do. Time is useless by itself and its main purpose is to help us easily remember a historical event. Time didn't exist until we created it. So time alone is not a remedy for all ills, it only isolates and quarantines the issue, until the time returns for it's application, and then it will either be suppressed or released as a wild beast. This is why I'm a firm believer that this judicial system fails us daily because if there isn't a conscious effort to rehabilitate today, society as a whole will continue to depreciate tomorrow.

It amazes me how off kilter our legal system is. It blows me away that citizens are steadily being used to pay the salaries for the manpower and resources to set up a drug sting to arrest "Shorty-g" and "lil moe." It's bewildering that we can pull out all the stops in spying on another country, traveling to the moon and building nuclear weapons but we seem incapable of being able to stop drugs from coming into our great country. I've been thinking extensively about this issue and its still ruff around the edges, but I've come up with a proposal. I propose that we take more than half of our drug agents that are implanted, and targeting the minority filled projects in our country, and remove them (in part) from that scene. Then we start asking our citizens for help again, because we know who's polluting our immediate areas. Yet, as long as it doesn't affect us directly then we let it go.

In most cases, the people that can help us the most often move out of the neighborhood. Next, Call on the strong men in our neighborhoods to videotape or patrol their own block, because if change is to come then it will have to be done jointly, by every capable and willing person of truth. Then, we take the law enforcement that we removed from the streets and place them across our coasts and have them start using all that technology and information that our great country has to offer to raid freighters and ships, that is if there's really a joint effort to rid our country of drugs. Sure, the local drug dealer would probably get away for the moment, but for the first time, a genuine effort will be taking place in order to take down the so-called "bigger fish", his supplier. The local hustler does not produce cocaine. Therefore, our forces will be concentrated at the core of the problem, while our citizens help the other 50% of enforcement on the home front. Everyone is held accountable now, and at the same time we finally have someone to police the police, with a magnifying glass.

Like I said, the plan is still rough around the edges, but it's a thought. It just hurts me to see our nation in such perils that it compels me to step up to the front line and fight. I don't think that it takes a rocket scientist because I'm definitely not one. All it takes is someone that seeks the truth and has a general love for all mankind.

The penal system affects us much, much deeper though. Let's look at it from a greater perspective. For every father that is incarcerated, there is a child that grows up without him. There's already a **70% ratio of African-American** women having children out of wedlock, and when we compound the distant father, by either being incarcerated or meeting an untimely death, the numbers are staggering. The deck is immediately stacked up against that child, with an incarcerated father, the mother is forced to take up both roles and if her career isn't already in full swing then her options can be disastrous in the long run. One option is welfare, which makes the family dependent on the state.

Another option is bringing another man into the picture, now it only makes the family dependent on that man, and in some cases it could also end in the abuse or fondling of your child. You never know the person that you're bringing into your home. The third, fourth and fifth options just keep getting worse and worse. Statistics show that a child without a male figure in the household is subject to all types of trials and tribulations and the odds of the child following in either the fathers or the mother's footsteps are severely high. *According to a study of 700 adolescents at www. protius.com researchers found that "compared to families with two natural parents living in the home, adolescents from single family homes have been found to engage in greater and earlier sexual activities."*

In cases of sexual abuse, in a study of *156* victims of child abuse found that the majority of abused children come from disrupted or single family homes. *31%* of the children lived with both biological parents and although stepfamilies make up only 10% of all families, *27%* of the abused children lived with either a stepfather or the mother's boyfriend. The same goes for drug, alcohol, and suicide rates. This information can be confirmed at "**Child Sexual Abuse Victims and Their Treatment**" *U.S. Department of Justice, Office of Juvenile Justice and Delinquency Prevention.* The incarceration, especially without rehabilitation destroys the family, the child, and society for generations to come because children (and lots

I mean think about it, he just looked up my anal, a place I haven't even seen before, and he made me take my hair down, and I hated it!

Many might think that the state gives us envelopes, soap, deodorant, toothpaste, or a toothbrush, but they don't. They give us ten dollars a month and if the institution goes on lockdown, then the monies for those days are confiscated, but on the flipside of that, the officers are paid time and a half. *From that $10 dollars that I hope to get, I must buy soap $2.00, toothpaste $2.00, deodorant $2.25, and envelopes are $.44.* Ten dollars barely gets me the necessities and on top of that, if for some reason I should ever need to go to the hospital (dental or medical department) it will cost me $2.00 for every trip. I know that ten dollars may not sound like a lot, but in there its all that we have, we consider those that have family with extra money to send them blessed. The institution that I was in doesn't even offer college courses, so the majority of the inmates are idle.

Many say, "man you're about to get out, I know you're happy as heck," and my answer is, "of course I am," but believe me when I say that as long as my family members are incarcerated then I can never be truly free! I actually feel that it was meant for me to see this first hand, because something has to be done to prevent this masquerade and I'm just the person to do it. I've seen all walks of life. I was raised in a broken household, on the streets of Chicago. I graduated high school, went to the Marine Corps, got married, worked a steady job as a railroad switchman, and went to jail. I've spent a significant amount of time with many different ethnic groups and my commitment to all of God's children is etched in my heart, so when I see how far blacks and Latinos are in this country as opposed to my white youth, it breaks that very same heart of mine in two. Life won't feel complete for me, until I bear witness to an even playing field for all of God's children.

There's no system in place to determine who's rehabilitated or not. The board can't possibly decide that in one visit per year. I found the motivation in myself to flourish, but believe me, look around you, our system is flawed and something has to be done. First and foremost, I feel as though rehabilitation should go hand in hand with your time and even when your sentence is done, if a change in attitude is not adjusted then, you should be held back, just like in school. On the other hand, if the teacher sees mass improvements then you should also be able to make a double as well. I'm not saying that it is a safe-proof plan, and I know that a few might feign the appearance of being rehabbed and slide through the format. That person would've been askew with or without the program, but imagine all of the crime that might be prevented by the program.

I'm open to suggestions, and I don 't care where the answers come from, as long as we obtain them; because that's all that matters. *I've stated several times that the system has failed us, but when we sit back and do nothing we fail ourselves!*

Chapter 7

Abortion

(Is it right or wrong?)

Such a complex question, such a serious matter, that even I don't know where I stand on the issue. The issue is far bigger than me so I believe that it is more important to open the floor for discussion rather than overlook it just because I don't have a solid opinion. Maybe, this chapter will spark the minds of others to the point where, not only do abortion rates drop but ,the pregnancy rate as well amongst unwed women and teenage girls. So many dreams have been altered or postponed and when abortions are performed, conscious minds are all left with the questions of, what if? Is it right? Is it wrong? So many families have been torn apart. So many daughters; young woman who have taken their own lives just because they were afraid of the response that they would receive from their mother or father (if he is around) after telling them that they were pregnant. These are precious lives with endless opportunity, cut short, all because of a pregnancy.

Before we even delve into the discussion of whether it's right or wrong, let's take it back to the stages that could've prevented the pregnancy all together. Parents, way before intercourse, pregnancy, and abortion became a thought, we should've been educating our children on the severe consequences of having unprotected sex. We know through experience that there are plenty of pitfalls that need to be avoided, many of which we may have fell victim to ourselves.

As a result, raising our children has been hard. When we were young we all dreamt of having kids and putting smiles on their faces. We couldn't wait to send them to college and then watch them raise their own families, but during the course of it all, life takes place and throws all types of curveballs. First, we have our children sooner than we expected and before we know it, we were forced to transform from adolescent to adulthood. Most of us weren't finish with high school so making a decent wage to take care of our children became a task in itself. Before we knew it, it was Christmas time, their birthday was near, and they were starting Pre School. They needed clothes, supplies, and more of your conscientious time. 8th grade graduation came about in a hurry and just like that your child was on their way to high school. Meanwhile, you're overwhelmed and filled all up with joy and one night as you drift into thought and try to figure out where all of the years went, you realize that you have no college savings set up for your child. It's a hurting feeling for a parent, because you know that there's nothing in the world that you wouldn't do for your child.

So with having said all of that, knowledge and wisdom is something that you will always have to give, it costs you nothing, so take advantage of the deal every chance that you can. Talk to your children and guide them along the right path, because we know the pressure that a young pregnant woman can feel. She feels alone, scared, overwhelmed, and unsure. Many young women have run away because of the stress. There are so many steps that could've been attempted before abortion became an option. Of course abstinence is the first choice and it should be emphasized to the fullest. Having experiences in life as a teenager already, we know that the statistics show that abstinence is not all that realistic. This is something that we have to face and suddenly all the hardship that we put our parents through is coming back around to torment us as parents. Next, protection should be addressed. Protection has become a major necessity these days because the threat of A.I.D.S and other sexually transmitted diseases is very real. There are contraceptives for woman as well as for men. Don't be nervous about having this conversation with your children. I've surveyed a lot of people and the number one thing that parents are afraid of, is bringing up the topic of sex, when their child previously didn't give it any thought. They're afraid of implanting the thought of sex into their child's mind, therefore making them curious to try it. I think that this thought process is incorrect, but could be true if we didn't live in a society where sex is advertised in all facets of life anyway. It's on every television network, some feature gay relationships that further complicates things (as far as a young child is concerned). (Girls gone wild) commercials air randomly. I'm to the point where I'm scared to rent a movie and watch it with my children for fear of what might be shown, regardless of the movie rating. It's all around us. Sex is selling everywhere, 24hrs a day. So I think that you're abandoning your children and doing them a disservice by opting not to have this conversation with them. If you don't take the time to teach them about sex, then society will, so take pride in nurturing your child with wisdom and knowledge.

Now once these walls of defense have been breached then we have no choice but to deal with the pregnancy. It is here that the thought of abortion becomes real in the minds of many, but the question still remains, is it right or is it wrong? What are the points of article behind our reasoning? Let's create some circumstances ourselves, and then think them over consciously, fair and impartial, Just as if we were the judge and jury presiding over the case. We have to hear all the facts, weigh them out properly and then make a sound judgment because life literally hangs on our decision.

First scenario, a young couple (around the age of 18) engages in unprotected sex and shortly after they find out that the girl is pregnant. After days of discussing the matter, the female decides that she doesn't want to have the baby and for reasons that she feels are legit. She's presently enrolled in college and momentarily being supported by her parents. Juggling pregnancy, along with the strenuous pressures of college, at this time, would be entirely too large of a load. The pregnant young lady has no income of her own, no transportation, and still remains two years away from graduation. She plays basketball for her college and is considered to be a future W.N.B.A. player. On the other hand, the father didn't go to college. He still makes a livable wage though, and he wants to have the baby for several reasons. He was told that he couldn't have children, so he has no idea if he will ever produce an embryo again. He offers to take the child into his custody and promises that the child will be provided for. On one hand we have a woman saying abort, and a man saying live; which way do we lean? Is it just so simple as to say that the woman should be entitled to have control over her body? I agree in part, because every individual is the master of their own body, and it belongs to them, and only them. Let's discuss this more thoroughly though.

When a man and woman come together in consensual, unprotected sex and create a fetus; it should be considered as a joint effort. A 50/50 partnership acknowledged by both. Therefore each of their opinions should be valued when it comes to any life that is created through the sexual act. I would argue that the woman still has 100% control over her body, because just as she consented to unprotected sex, she also had the opportunity at that point to still say no. Its only after engaging in the sexual act that I feel as though both parties should have some say so when it comes to any life produced from it. How could it not, when neither person could create or produce a child (naturally) by him/her self. So how do we vote in this type of scenario? Is it just to be written in stone, that the woman has the final say so? Are we literally decreasing the man down to a sperm donor? *I know a few women that would say that it's been like that for some time now.* Is it correct to say that the man has no rights? I agree wholeheartedly that it is the female's body. By not protecting herself against pregnancy though, I wouldn't say she necessarily gave up her rights to her body, but where the fetus is concerned, the authority should be shared in my most humble opinion. It's shared in every other facet of the child's upbringing, so why not when it comes to the birth of the child? When the child is born, the father is ordered by law to pay for the necessities of the child he helped to create. I'm in 100% agreement with that because it's morally and spiritually sound. It's a gift given to you by the creator.

Besides that, It is morally right for a man to not only financially support his child, but to be their mentally to teach him how to be a man that respects women and teaches other men to be men. With all this in consideration, why shouldn't the young man be able to have say so on whether his child receives a chance at life or not?

Let's say that we agree that the authority is 50/50, how do we rule with our scenario? Would it violate the woman's rights to have her carry out the pregnancy and delivery just to turn custody over to the father or, does it violate the man's rights by saying that only the woman's opinion counts. Well if we vote in favor of the abortion, we are saying that the woman does overrule the man in this situation. If we rule on the side of the man, then it could be argued that the woman's point of view is overlooked. All I want to do in this chapter get us all to look at it from the baby's perspective! What if we reverse the roles and the man is in college on his way to the N.B.A and the woman is at a decent job. Now, the man wants to abort the fetus and the woman wants to keep her child because she was told that she could never have kids. In her eyes, this child is a miracle. Now which way do you rule? The most important question I have is, did your vote for abortion or life change? If so, why? Was it because of who wanted to keep the baby this time and who didn't? If man and woman are considered by all to be equal, then this line of thinking has to stop. It can't be men against woman, or men for men, or women for women. The decisions have to be based on what's morally the right thing to do.

Would our reasoning swing again if the mother was homeless and lived on lower wacker drive in Chicago and the father was unknown? Could we understand this woman's reasoning for wanting an abortion? On the other hand, would we object to her living on the streets amongst rats and all sorts of diseases while planning on having the baby? What if it were two people that had epilepsy or autism and they were expecting a child, but the (parents) of both young adults thought it to be a bad idea because of the amount of commitment, reasoning, and patience it takes to care for the baby, better yet the child. If the parents die, who will take over this responsibility? These are just some of the scenarios that could play out. How would you rule?

Going back to our first examples, like I said, I don't have all the answers but I do think that changes need to come about, because there of times adults) need a pattern in life to follow. If there isn't a positive one around more than likely the negative one will be pursued.

Rehabilitation is the gist of my conversation. Of course, it would be beautiful to rid the country completely of crime but until utopia takes full form, an affective plan must be in place. The jail staff goes over and beyond the call of duty on certain areas, the miniscule ones, but lack a complete effort in the major ones. Once the judge sentences the guilty, the punishment is administered as proven in the previous paragraphs. Yet in still, the security guards, that basically turn keys and baby sit us, feel as though it's their place to determine whether or not each individual is doing hard time or not. If only they knew that "*anytime*" away from ones family is hard time. They go to extra measures to show their superiority and it gets so bad at times, it feels like slavery in a modern way though. As I look into the officer's eyes, I can see the insecurity in him. It's as if he can't understand how I'm able to deal with the adversity of being locked up and still have the pride and heart to look him in his eyes.

Whenever a white female officer would speak to me, the white male officers faces would become bright red- As if they yearned to put me back in my proper place. As if they'd heard all of the slavery stories from their grand parents, and longed for the opportunity to experience it. In these days, *him* being an officer and *I* being a prisoner is the closest they will ever come to *modern day slavery*. They abuse their power just to appease their own self-consciousness. They try to humiliate us every chance they get, especially if it's in front of a female officer, white or black.

I understand the reasons that security measures must be in place, but it is very demoralizing when the officer says, " Cooke, visit." I would get ready thinking about the feeling that will come over me once I embrace my family, then as I make it to the visiting room the officer says "take your braids down, they're not allowed." I asked "why not, why is it mandatory that I have to go in front of my family unshaved, with a low morale level?" He said, "those are the rules, pants down, turn around and bend over, now Spread'em!" I'm like, "what the hell could I actually be smuggling out of the institution to my family, through my anal passage." Then after that he said, "Have a nice visit." "How can I, and you just visually raped me?"

are so many other things that could factor into the equation. For one, it puzzles me that we give the illusion that a fetus isn't a human being until the time of birth, at least, that's the way it seems. Why is it that the child's birthday is one year from the date of delivery rather than the day of actually becoming a human being? So the question is, when is the embryo or fetus considered a being, when the arms, legs, and head forms, or is it when the heart forms, how do we determine this? This topic furthers my thought because if we're discussing when it is that a fetus is considered a human being; we also have to discuss the point at which a fetus feels pain. Does the fetus feel pain when an abortion takes place and if so, then how can it not be considered murder? How could it not? The circumstances of the woman or man's life should not justify murder. Some may argue, that it's not murder, that's too harsh of a word; well *it is what it is*. For example, if a man kills a woman and during the autopsy it is discovered that the woman was pregnant, then that man will not only be charged for the murder of the woman, but also for the murder of the fetus, showing clearly that the fetus is considered a human. Whatever the mother eats, the fetus eats. Whatever the mother feels, the fetus also feels.

The fact that there is a being inside the mother can't be denied. So, if the man is charged with killing a fetus, then the mother should be too for taking the child's life in any fashion. That is if we are agreeing that the fetus is a being? If we are to agree that abortion is wrong? Now, if abortion is to be a legal thing, then some form of when and why should be defined. Something has to be done because these are lives that will never get the chance to prosper. If an abortion is to take place then, I feel as though it should be agreed upon; by both parents. If a mother comes in requesting an abortion, then the assumed father's consent should be obtained. If there is one parent that wants an abortion and one that does not, then the pregnancy should be fulfilled. The child will go on to be raised by the active parent who chose to support them. I know that this might not be the best, but at least it's a start in the right direction. I know that there are other circumstances as well, for example, if a woman is raped and forced to have sexual intercourse, I feel as though she should have the right to have an abortion. The downside to this is that we'd have plenty of women claiming a false rape, delaying the process of true and serious cases.

There are so many conversations that can arise from this topic, several of them. For instance, if we come together and say that to receive the birth of a child is gift, then what we're saying is that life has been given, by the Creator, and that it should be cherished, honored, and revered. Therefore, by this theory, it is hard to understand how some scientist's can come together for the practice of cloning a human or an animal. It's an unnatural process for creating so called life. We're manipulating the process of divine intervention and it's no better than ending the life of an embryo, that is, the act of creating life without a natural embryo.

There are so many complicated issues. It almost feels unfair to demand a mother carry a baby she didn't want for 9mths, if the father is willing to nurture and care for the child, taking the life of the fetus seems even worse. As far as the father is concerned, I'm willing to enforce the law if a father reneges on his commitment to taking over the rights of his child. It should be a class x felony if a father doesn't live up to his promises, punishable by jail time. I know that some may frown upon this, but what should be frowned upon is men/boys that implant these seeds into woman and then turn around and don't support them after birth. The fact that men have to be forced to take care of their children is askew and deplorable. I can't think of any crime worse than a man not taking care of his child.

I know that some of my proposals might need more work, but I think that we can agree that we're in a state now were more work is a good thing, cause it's needed anyway. I understand that it will be nearly impossible to establish the paternity of a child in the early stages of pregnancy, but somehow some way we have to start taking responsibility for our actions. I realize that a woman might live her life as several men do and have multiple partners. In this case, all of her sex partners should be notified that they could possibly be the father and if one of those men decide that they would want the birth of their possible child to take place then the pregnancy must be fulfilled, a condition that should be met following the woman's decision of having unprotected sex with several men, in the same time period. If the child turns out not to be that of the man who wanted this birth to take place, then he is not bound by law to still raise the child. By this time, after delivery, and the mother has seen the pretty smile of her babies face, just maybe the mother might reconsider, and if not, then in this case the child would go into the custody of an immediate family member, and the state as a final result. If none of the men's test match the DNA, then the mother should be incarcerated, for having irresponsible sex and endangering a child's rights to know their father. Only if the father is deceased does the mother have full authority of deciding the fate of her child.

The point of this chapter is that we should take serious the fact that unnecessary lives have been terminated before they even started, unable to even make their own decision, unable to dream or aspire. We can't continue this type of practice.

So remember, protect yourself if you engage in sexual encounters and never downplay the fact that this is an actual life that we're ending, in its earliest stages. Let's try and work together to decrease the overwhelming amount.

Chapter 8

Excel in life

(Maximizing you 24hr day)

Learn from yesterday and prepare for tomorrow by making the correct moves today. If you come from middle to lower class, I can totally relate with you. We had no college funds set aside. We were taught no financial skills, and the daily pressures of life just made it hard to enjoy today. One of the reasons for these financial straits is because of broken households. Out of the ten friends that I had growing up as a child, only two of them had a mother and father in the house, and out of those two, only one of the fathers made a significant income. It's almost impossible to have financial success when only one parent is pulling in an income that is utilized to take care of a complete family. The economic system is structured and built around the idea of a family functioning off of two solid incomes.

Now you're the adult, and whether with or without kids, you probably live like I use to, paycheck to paycheck. Nobody left me any money in a will and if I decided to give in and succumb to the pressures of the world, no one would blame me. In fact, no one expected anything out of me, nobody accept the person that counted, and that's me.

The first thing that needed to be adjusted was not my bank account or my current pay wage, but my mentality. I had to come to the realization that I was utilizing my knowledge and information, learned earlier in my life, incorrectly. The point of the matter is that I had become to engulfed and soaked in my own sorrow. I was drowning in it and I felt as though it was someone else's responsibility to, not only fix the problem but; acknowledge and broadcast to the world that I was given a raw deal. That would've made me feel great! I figured out quickly that life doesn't work that way; it's just not that forgiving, even to a race of people that had experienced the worst form of oppression ever applied to a group of people in life. So instead of focusing in on the parts of the past that would continue to keep me handcuffed, I started to focus in on what is was that could be done differently on my part in order to better my situation and solidify my children's future.

By learning from the past, I already had a list of things that didn't work. If I just made a conscious effort not to make those mistakes again, the chances of me reversing this cycle increases almost instantaneously. It might not be the quickest route, but through trial and error the truth of success will be revealed. The first step to reversing a negative *motif* is focusing on past events/mistakes, only for the purpose of not making them again. The knowledge of past events is one of the most valuable assets that you can have. For instance, if you buy a car with an interest rate of 20%, and afterwards you find out that 6% is a more reasonable rate. Chances are you won't make that mistake again, conversely, self-teaching yourself through trial and error.

It wasn't the most efficient route, but you eventually arrived at greater reasoning. Now, if you took the lesson and applied it to every other thing in your life, it would make you that much more successful and a master of our first rule, and that is looking at past mistakes only for the purpose of avoiding the same mistakes in the future. To even further utilize this rule of thumb, realize that your learning process is not just subjected to your mistakes, because you can actually learn more by taking notes from others mistakes (situations). It's quicker and less painful (financially and mentally) to observe the outcome of others that have went before us, especially for circumstances like the one previously mentioned. Had we taken a tad bit of time to survey multiple car dealers then, we could have come up with an average interest rate for a car. Newspapers and word of mouth would've proved useful as well. Now it seems simple with a situation like that, it seems like common sense. It appears to be the instinctive thing to do, but when the pressures of life take place and you're receiving stress from all angles; work, the kids and etc. your decision making process can become clouded.

For example, as a kid we were taught good characteristics traits like, never starting a fight, but if forced to; then definitely finishing it. Protect yourself at all times. That's definitely good information, but why is it that more emphasis (over the years) is placed on teaching kids how to fight than it is on avoiding and neutralizing a problem? My point is that, it's only through trial and error that we finally realize that we only get one body and the heart not being directly equivalent to the engine of a car, can't be continuously replaced like an engine can, after the last one fails. You only get one life. You don't have nine lives and there is only one way to be born; yet there are countless ways to die. It's with all of this understanding that we realize that life is to short to waste it on minor things such as fighting and arguing. When the situation is directly in your face, in real time, it's very difficult to reflect on others mistakes and remove yourself from the problem. The scenario is quite more intense than finding a car to buy.

Secondly, try not to procrastinate when it comes to shooting toward your goals, because the more you procrastinate, the more your percentages of actually completing your task decreases. Just think about it, how many times have you thought about going back to school? How many times have you put off writing your book? What about marriage, saving for a house, or learning to speak another language? All it takes to complete either of these tasks is for you to take the first step. The first step is always the hardest mountain to climb throughout the process. Some of the dedication and commitment might seem overbearing at times, but yet in still, you will continue to press forward because you can actually see yourself improving. You instantaneously start receiving the fruits of your labors, defeating the restraints of procrastination is the driving force behind me completing my dream of writing this book. The one thing that I had to continuously pound in my head was that it was never too late to chase my dreams. I repeatedly got caught up with the age factor, letting my own conscious hold me back. Self-doubt also played a part until I realized that time stops for no man and that no one can achieve my goal for me, but me. A year from today, whether I pursue my dream or not, I will in fact become a year older.

There's nothing that can stop that, so since time will elapse regardless I might as well take the time to achieve all that I can, if not for myself, then for my children. Once I took that approach, procrastination became like a state of vegetation to me, as I sat back and watched the world go round. The options were endless once I got started and the same will be for you. Before you know it, you'll be that much closer to graduating just take it a class at a time, just do it. If you're a person that has put off for years writing your book, just do yourself a favor, as soon as you finish reading this, start on yours. Beat procrastination by taking the first step. Get the witch off of your back and just do it. Also, remember your book is your thoughts and it doesn't have to be perfect the first time around. No one's book ever is, that's why it's called a rough draft, before publishing it, trust me. You will rewrite your book over and over, making it better and better.

Here's a tip also, try picking up a pen and forcing yourself to write nonstop for at least a minute straight. It can't hurt you; all it can do is benefit you in your quest. It can't harm you at all, because if there's something in there that you don't like then you can always throw it away. It costs you nothing but a tad bit of time, one minute, two minutes, or whatever time that you allot for your mission, so just do it. You will thank yourself in the end and once you start your mission, you're guaranteed to ask yourself, "What took so long." You will be filled up with all sorts of self worth, and gratification. You will be surprised on what a step like this will do for your confidence level in general. You will enhance your self worth by beginning to seize all moments and when it comes to dating, you are prone to look for this (new found) characteristic trait in the other person as well. It's one thing that we know for sure though, that if we just give it a go then the sky is the limit. If you let your age and general procrastination compel you to do nothing then, your rewards in life will be equivalent to your effort. So always learn from the past and never ever procrastinate.

Thirdly, this may sound cliché' or quaint but, I promise you that it will work. You've done it before, but never really stuck to it, I'm talking about writing down a priority list. Listen, its one thing to have an agenda and a set of goals. It's a totally different thing to wake up every morning to the same writings on the wall. It almost forces you to hold yourself accountable for the goals that you set for yourself. At Notre Dame, before every game, they have to touch a sign on the wall that says, "*play like champions*". In offices around the nation you have these sayings and all types of *aphorisms* posted on the wall or taped to desks and it works. It's a proven marketing tool, as stated in our previous chapter entitled economics.

When I was in the military, the up coming days were already planned. We knew exactly what was expected of us on a daily basis and we used every ounce of energy to meet that quota. This mentally accomplished many things for us as far as our individual growth was concerned. For one, it kept us busy and always positively reaching for our goals, leaving no room for us to dwell on negative things and it directly opposed procrastination. Secondly, by the time our work was done, we were so tired that relaxation and sleep was all that the rest of the day held for us. Having a priority list gave me goals to complete and on a daily bases it instilled me with the feeling of self worth to the point that the characteristic became instinctively a part of me. Remember that the architect draws the building plans and designs before he actually builds the building, and when building your future, so should you. The art of prioritizing and having a set agenda have proven to be a wise and successful trait. Go to any fortune 500 Fortune company meeting and you will see that they have what is called a strategic plan that is covered over a number of years. It states that in one year, two years, or in five years, this is where our company is projected to be. Detailed inside these files is how it's going to happen in stages and if it doesn't, someone will be held accountable, so prioritizing it will ensure that every step you take is toward success.

Fourth, surround yourself with people who not just aspire to have more tomorrow than what they did today, but with people who actually put forth the efforts to make it happen. Surround yourself around people that are doers, because as the old adage goes, if you surround yourself around nine successful people then you are bound to be the tenth. You have to branch off and put yourself in the position to be successful. Although it would make for a warm and heartfelt story, the probability of all your associates having the same dreams and work ethics as you is highly unlikely. Therefore, you have to meticulously choose your circle because, out of 10 associates that you have, you're lucky if one of them is a true friend of yours. My point is that just because someone is an associate, doesn't necessarily mean that they equate to good business partners. There's three different mentalities, *stagnate minds* remain stationary sitting back and watching as the world goes round, while discussing the things that other people are doing with their lives. Then there are *average mentalities* that discuss (without ever acting upon it) what they could possibly be tomorrow, while the food off of their plates are being eaten, today, by another. The *extraordinary mind* discusses his role in future events by seizing the opportunities allotted to them today. They become involved in the affairs of men. They understand that people don't become successful by merely wishful thinking. So they ask themselves one question, how did they become successful? Two, what are they doing that I'm not? Three, once they became successful; how did they sustain that level?

The fourth and final step is, utilizing every resource at your disposal. So many people skip over the simple things, incapable of seeing the pure beauty within them. All you have to do is stop looking with your eyes and use your heart and mind. You want to learn about metaphysics and the laws of nature? Sure, you can scan the web and do research in the library, but don't forget about your number one resource, which would be an older and wiser person in your family. You get an element from them that can't be fully obtained from a textbook. For example, its one thing to read about the civil rights movement, but it's another thing all together to sit down and listen to someone who marched with Martin Luther King Jr. tell you about the setting and temperament. It's almost equivalent to knowing that animals are killed for their fur coating, elephants for their ivory trunks, and all sorts of animals for food but, it's a whole different perspective when you actually witness the unnecessary slaughter.

You have to take advantage of all that wisdom and knowledge when it comes to your children. You should make time for them, seize the moment, take your babies for a walk to the park, set aside a family day, it doesn't matter what you all do as long as you take that time to bond. You can play basketball in the driveway, you can go to the batting cages, a live baseball game, or you can just stay home and play Pictionary or Monopoly. It really doesn't matter because the most important thing is that you connected with your children, and they will always remember that. It's within these moments that you can take the time to teach your kids about abstinence or protecting themselves. You can take the time to teach them about the dangers of smoking and the reasons why it's important to call home if they're going to be late for their curfew (My daughter is still going to be in trouble, but you get the point). You might think that they're not listening, but you'd be surprised. I can remember vividly the things that my grandmother taught me, and she reiterated them so much that when the persuasion of peer pressure came in my direction; I could literally hear the lessons that my grandmother instilled in me playing itself out in my head. I still have those lessons with me today, small conversations that took place at the dinner table or while we were watching the cubs play on W.G.N. let's go cubbies, yeah I said it! If you're mad write your own book and root for your team.

Even after my grandmother's burial, the values that she bestowed in me will allow her to live forever. Spend time with your children while they're young before you're faced with the harsh reality that your kids are grown up, and now (while in your older age) they don't have time for you.

These four steps should be utilized to there fullest capacity when dealing with anything in life. If you strategize correctly you can prepare for job interviews with a clearer understanding of what they expect out of you. Remember that the interviewee always has the upper hand on the interviewer because they know absolutely nothing about you (besides what's on the application) so the interview is set up to learn more and go into depth about you and your qualifications. On the other hand, you have the time to study everything about the company that you've applied for by:

1. Learn form the past. You know that you'll be asked what makes you qualified for this position? Where did you previously work and why did you choose this company? It would be in your best interest to have the answers to those questions.

2. Never procrastinate. If it's a position that you want to apply for, but you're not 100% sure that you'll get it, or whether you meet the criteria, fill out the forms anyway. Even if you don't get the position, at least you'll know what it is you need to do in order to better prepare yourself for the position.

3. Lists your priorities, therefore, once you get your new job, you'll never forget the reasons why you needed it in the first place. A priority list will inevitably keep you on a straight and narrow path saving you a lot of financial heartache along the way. A priority list can combat stress, because something that couldn't even make your priority list should never be able to cause you to have restless and sleepless nights.

4. Stay surrounded by positive people. They can help you in finding a solid job therefore you'll also have credible references to add to your application. Last but not least, by completing all of those moves, you will also be utilizing all of your resources. This method works with whatever you apply it to.

Seizing the moment is, understanding that opportunity will never just come knocking on your door. It's a metaphor that has been misconstrued. It's an illusion and the only way to be successful is for you to walk up and knock on the door of opportunity, and if no one answers, you have to be willing to kick the hinges off of the door. You have to be able to show everyone why they can't afford to pass on you. Everyday is an opportunity for higher learning so take advantage of that. Look at everyone going about there business. Think about what it is you want to do and then observe a person in that field go about their daily business. It'll help you in your quest significantly.

The past, present, and future are all a part of you. It's the theme of this chapter. *Learning from yesterday, preparing for tomorrow, and most importantly making the correct moves today. Excel in life from here on out!*

Chapter 9

Our Community

(It still takes a village)

What happened? Where did we lose our morals, values, and apathy for our brother's adversity? Where did we go wrong? Where did we lose our sense of urgency, and what can we do to get it back?

As African Americans, we've had a very tough road to travel. Even at our darkest hour, at our lowest lows, we never lost respect and love for one another. It's as if we're under the impression that we've crossed some sort of finish line. As if all of our legwork has been done. *This island of relaxation off of the shores is merely a mirage that disappears as soon as you dive into it, leaving you drenched in nothing but a dose of reality.* It pains me to see the state that we're in. Even worse, it eats me up internally to know that I've previously contributed to these woes and ills. Like many, I was blinded by fool's gold incapable of seeing the annihilation that was falling upon and plaguing our communities.

Not so long ago, we could blame our dismal and dire situations on the oppression received by others and would be justified. The accusation would've been right and exact, but this is a new era and time, now opportunities are afforded to us. Are there still wrongs being committed, is there still racism, is prejudice still being practiced? Without a doubt! What's changed is that we no longer have to accept the conditions. We can fight back, mentally, with education at the forefront of the battle. If we're ever to become involved in the affairs of men tomorrow, then we have to stand up and take responsibility for ourselves today. Understand that those who meet at the round table to discuss what is best suited for the whole of society are those that have let it be known that they are capable of standing independently in society. It wasn't until black people fought for and obtained the right to vote (which would sway the outcome of an election) that either party considered listening to their complaints.

In other words, if you're tired of the drug problem in your neighborhood, if you're tired of the senseless deaths of children *(in the 2006-2007 school year alone twenty-eight kids were slain in Chicago, IL.) 500 since that time, which leads the nation.* Then, you have to become pro-active and get involved in the affairs of men. We have to take our communities back and put a greater emphasis on the lives of our children. Avoid the *nay sayers* because those that don't have the drive to complete the mission, have not the right to question those who do. These are some of the same principles that the Civil Rights movement was founded on. Fried determination and a yearning for righteousness made it necessary. To put it in the words of my grandmother, "if you're waiting for someone else to bring you joy, happiness, and peace, then you better not hold your breath".

Speaking of grandmothers, it brings me to my first point of interest when trying to rationalize how and where we went wrong and how do we correct it. When we talk of uplifting a community, collectively it starts with each family, individually building upon the principles of love, mercy, justice, and everything that is right. Grandparents are at the epicenter of that building process. They are the corner stone of our families. Just as the pastor of a church can unite and uplift a whole congregation; so do the grandparents of our families. Grandparents love unconditionally. As stated previously, I wish that my grandfather would've taken the time out to teach me a trade; such as mechanic, mason, or electrician. By giving me these skills, he would've instilled key components within me. For one, he would've given me something that could be passed on from generation to generation. Two, he would've taught me that with hard work I could learn anything in the world. My confidence level would've been soaring, a critical step to success.

Now my grandmother, she was my confidant, my heart, and my life support system. We came to spend the weekend with grandma all of the time and it was here that our values and morals were honed. There was no such thing as wearing a hat in my grandma's house. She always told me that it was a sign of respect for a person to take their hat off when entering someone else's domicile. Sagging pants was a no-no. She taught me that there's nothing like a man who dresses neat and is clean cut. At grandma's house we all received plenty of love, likewise with discipline. At an early age we knew that certain things were required of us; we all had chores and we were held accountable for them. Unaware of what was taking place, I thought we had chores, just because, but in reality; character was being developed in us. Being able to take orders, listen, and efficiently complete tasks would turn out to be priceless. I knew automatically that our German Sheppard named chink had to be walked twice a day at specific times. One person was responsible for setting the table for dinner, washing the dishes, and etc. My grandmother's house is where I learned to say my prayers, in which she wrote down and dared me not to know them within 24hrs. She was fine tuning me for life outside of our house by giving me exactly what the world would; hard times and no second chances. After she was finished for the day, she would always close it by giving us plenty of love the same way the day began, thus finalizing her last lesson of the day. She did all of this because she cared. She cared enough to prepare me for what the future had in store.

Equipped with the tools that grandma gave us, we were then prepared to positively contribute to our community. It's similar to the 'Gestalt School of Thought advanced by Max Wertheimer, a German psychologist, who emphasized the study of thinking and perception in whole units opposed to analyzing experiences into parts, possibly inventing the slogan, "the whole is greater than the sum of it's parts". Dennis Coon in the introduction to psychology described it as such. Imagine that you played,

"Happy Birthday" on a tuba and then played it on a high pitch violin. The sound from the tuba and violin are different, yet the melody is completely recognizable. Now, what would happen if you put the notes of the "Happy Birthday" song in the correct order but, at a rate of one note per hour, then what would you have? Little of nothing, thus supporting the claim that the separate notes would no longer be a melody. The perception is that the (whole) melody is somehow more than the individual notes that define it. Can you now see how important the community is, as a whole, versus one household in particular?

The problem that we have now a days is that the grandmother of today is much younger, and still in the process of living her own life; chasing her dreams, therefore engulfing time that use to be spent for the growth and development of the young child. All of the other topics in this book play their role, but I beg of you grandmother's, please take our families back because we need you. Grandfathers, play your roles as well. Get involved with the development of your grandchildren. Set examples to the boys of what a man should be and set an example to the girls of what a real man should encompass. All in all, I long for the day that our grandparents once again stay together through thick and thin and give us a picture of what love can become.

Mothers and fathers; began to purchase single-family homes. While the grandparents remain the glue of the entire family, it's our duty and obligation to take control of our independent families. No one is excused nor will they be relieved of their position. Everyone has a role to play.

Young men, first and foremost we need to redefine what it means to be a man. Most of us, being void of a father all of our lives and never get a chance to see firsthand what it takes to completely be a man, so we're forced to obtain information from elsewhere. Our fathers are abandoning their posts, therefore, allowing the enemy, the streets (and all that it entails) to infiltrate and defect our children. In the streets, it's every one for themselves. We throw the term "its love" or "it's all good" around loosely, but believe me when I say, "ain't no love" because everything has gone bad. Its survival of the fittest out there and in the words of Grandmaster Flash and the Furious Five, *"it's like a jungle sometimes it makes me wonder how I keep from going under."* You have to fight and fend off predators to prevent from being swallowed whole. Subconsciously, the seed is planted that one of the characteristics of being a man is engaging in physical confrontation. It is believed that all problems can be solved that way. Now you have everyone fighting for supremacy with no one willing to back down. Where a fight would usually solve a problem, more serious tactics have been implemented, and taking another man's life is not above approach.

That type of mentality has an amazing negative rippling effect on our society though. Not only does one of the two fighting individuals possibly loose their life, but the other one will go to jail for the rest of his life immediately affecting both of those families. On top of that, these two men also served as the role model for the rest of the young men who unfortunately had to turn to the street for guidance. This macho and egotistical mentality is killing us from the inside out, because once that tactic is embedded into the psyche, it becomes a behavioral pattern and unlike a light switch, it can't be turned on and off. Now you have a multitude of young men, stemming from the root of a few, who will carry these characteristic traits back to their house, school, job site, and into any relationship that they encounter.

They only know one way of solving problems, and it's in the extreme way. When these young men get into confrontations in high school, in which way do you think they'll respond? How will they handle a boss that demands for a job to be completed by the end of the night? How will they respond to a girlfriend that disagrees with them? Physical violence towards the people in these scenarios is not a stretch.

Our sisters look for a partner in our men. They expect us to be leaders, fathers, and loyal husbands but so far, we've been failing them. We applaud our women when they dress overly seductive. We deceive them and put together *clandestine* plans to satisfy our lower self. Once a woman gives herself to them, we then label them bitches and hoes, there's no consistency in that. The only thing that remains consistent is inconsistency. Men equate physical dominance with total dominance over another and that is *erroneous*. It's clear that our young sons don't know what it takes to be a complete man, because they never had a positive prototype to follow. This is where our fathers come into play.

Father's, when you abandon your obligations you leave a mother to *"act"* as a father, and you leave a son to turn to the streets for a male role model. Whether we recognize it or not, our sons and daughters will find leadership from somewhere. Fathers, you leave your sons with no knowledge of how to treat a woman. Young men go deep into there adulthood before they even see another man love a woman mind, body, and soul.

Between the ages of two and three are critical for the early childhood development of our sons and daughters. Fathers, you need to spend time with your sons. Teach them how to brush their teeth, catch a baseball, and show courtesy to all people. You should teach those ethics, morals, and other things such as putting a tie on correctly or reading and writing. So to all you fathers out there, spend time with your children tonight. If they don't live with you, call them and if you don't have contact with your children, then put it on the top of your priority list to correct that.

Mothers its time we start paying more attention to our daughters, because the young woman of today are our grandmothers of tomorrow. Without an active mother, young girls find themselves in the same dilemma as young men, because they have to turn to other young girls for guidance, most of which didn't have active mothers in their lives either. We have young men who haven't the least idea of how to treat a woman or connect with her. These young girls (by not receiving the proper knowledge and intelligence from their mothers) tend to absorb the false sense of security from men in the street. Many become so dependent on the men that sex is the only way of feeling self worth. There are women that show little, or no discretion amongst the amount of men that approach their doorstep. Nor are they conscious of the fact that their daughters are taking note of every move. The daughter will have the propensity to choose the same type of men that her mother did. The actions that the man displayed with the child's mother will appear to be the norm for that child, unless that action is combated.

I know that there is a lot of pressure on the mothers of today. Most women became mothers at early ages, so they are trying desperately to juggle raising their children, along with jumpstarting their career, while at the same time fulfilling the role and duty of the irresponsible father. Stay strong though mothers, because you are still the cornerstone of our families, and your daughter deserves to see an independent woman like you stand strong in the face of adversity. Once she grows older, she won't need a man to validate her strength. She will be upright, independent, and fearless upon her own traits that she learned from you. On behalf of every man that has ever brought a woman pain or neglected their duty to their children, I apologize with the deepest sincerities. It's something about having a daughter that makes you see the world differently.

Everything is affected by these alpha male and sovereign mentalities, just look around you. In years past, people were just trying to keep up with the Jones' but nowadays, it's all about out *being* the Jones' which feeds directly to our narcissistic traits. The need to stand at the top of a mountain and look down on others is killing us at an unbelievable rate. It's a false sense of security. It lies to us and it's a psychological disease that is deteriorating our bodies. Those that say, "I'm just doing me," probably mean it when they say it but they just don't realize how their brains have been programmed to think that way. They say that they dress for themselves, buy cars for themselves, along with rims and jewelry, but subconsciously, they also know that they will receive praise from others who incorrectly worship these material items. They will be exalted and held high because of this false status and who can deny the large amount of attention that will come from the opposite sex. At first, it was 10"rims, 13," 14," 15," (standard issued).

Then there was 17", 18", 19", 20," (dubs)! 24", 25,"26," When is it going to stop? It's the same as the scenario I pointed out earlier when you have two bold, cynical, and egotistical people battling for the thrown on the top of the mountain. They will stop at nothing to obtain it. It's a fight to the death. How many times have you heard of someone being killed for there rims, jewelry, or money? These all are false gods that we've been deceived into idealizing. The worst part is that we want to do better. We only want to live without suffering and starving, but the route we're taking is just not the best. It's like we have the right idea, the correct amount of determination and will, but we're just climbing up the wrong mountain. We have brothers that will stand in line all night to get the last tickets for a playoff game, and people will kill to get certain drugs, clothing, or jewelry. It's the right determination and will, but the wrong mountain. Just imagine if we had that same amount of brothers in line, not for tickets to a game, but for the purpose of protecting our kids on their way back and forward from school. *While I'm at it, I would be remised if I didn't acknowledge Chi Town's very own Guardian Angels. They are comprised of strong black fathers who take to the street to protect our youth on their way to and from school, and they have been around since I was a kid. NOW, THAT'S WHAT'S UP!*

Even if men are no longer with the mother of their child, please take care of your children. Just imagine if these brothers were lined up to pick their children up to spend quality time with them or possibly buy them school supplies. How much better would we be as a society?

I know that life is hard for us. I come from the east side of Chicago, and I've seen poverty. I know how to boil water in order to have a hot bath. I've eaten government cheese, sliced it (as hard as that is), and cooked bologna until it bubbled in the middle, and all that. Sometimes, we feel suppressed and closed in, but we have to remember that your brother (next door) is not responsible for your current situation. We have to come together and support our black businesses instead of acting like crabs in a barrel. It seems as if every time a brother or sister makes it to the top of the pot, right on the verge of leaving the pits of poverty, here comes one of the crabs to pull them back down. Misery loves company and if it weren't for misery, a many of people wouldn't have anything else to do today.

We have to break these stereotypes and start holding each other accountable for the uplifting of our community. For far too long, we've set back and accepted the title of, "products of our environment." For far too long we've accepted that excuse especially when it came to goals that required a lot of effort. Most of the time we're not scared to fail, we're scared to succeed, so instead of attempting the goal we sit back and do nothing. Afterwards, we exercise our privilege to the term, "product of the environment" always leaving us with the space to say, "Only if I had the same opportunities as others". We never had it easy. We've never had equal rights, and that's not a secret. The secret is exactly what it is that we're going to do about it. Can someone please tell me?

We come from poverty, a place where people have prayed to God so long that they've turned atheist. We come from a place where we don't know what's better protection, God or guns. We are in a state of emergency. We have work to do, mothers and fathers let us take our communities back.

The violence and hatred has forced a justified distrust amongst us. It's caused us to divide, therefore becoming that much easier to conquer. There is no generational gap with us. There's just a gap between our communications with one another. We've failed our young brothers and sisters tremendously. We have let them raise themselves, and we've instilled them with no values. I remember when I was a young kid and there was an emphasis placed on a man being able to make a legitimate dollar to support his family. So as a teenager, we thought of constructive and legal ways to make our money. Plus, the environment still allowed us to be children. Back then, parents didn't have to fear letting there children go to the park and play as much as they have to in these days and times. Early in the morning on a Saturday or Sunday, me and my friends would get together and sit at the grocery store and every time someone came out, we would ask them if they needed help carrying their bags to their car or to their house. I guess that people were so happy to see some young brothers doing something productive that they didn't hesitate to take us up on our offer, and then they would give us a quarter, fifty-cents, and sometimes more. Then we would take the lawnmower and go around cutting people's grass, we came around so often that some people became regular customers. Every Saturday I'd make sure that I cut Mrs. Thompson's grass first because she was the first to ever give me a chance. We did the same with every season whether fall or winter. We raked leaves and shoveled snow not even realizing that we were basically running our own landscaping business. Not to mention, learning and exercising characteristic traits that would be utilized every single day of our lives.

After we received our fee for our services, we immediately turned back to kids and spent it all at the game room and candy store. If I had two dollars, I got four solid quarters one to play Ms. Pac-man, Galaga, Centipede, and Tron. That was my thing right there. Everyone around my age knows what I'm talking about too; stop playing. Then I would use the other dollar for twenty-five pink cookies twenty-five big blows, some now and laters, lemonheads, cherry-chans, and chi-co-sticks. Then, we would all get together to buy a soft ball; or rubber coated ball to play strikeout with. Piggy one, two, three was our favorite game with the softball. We would get the bat and ball and then call, "piggy one, piggy two, piggy three". "Piggy one" was the batter, "two" was the pitcher, and "three" was the catcher. Everybody else played in the field. Once the ball was pitched and the batter hit it, it had to either be fielded on a fly ball on one bounce. The beauty of it was that you could set your own rules, so if we had a lot of girls from the neighborhood that wanted to play then we would change it to two bounces. It entertained us for hours, just as *off the wall* did. In this game, we used a tennis ball and bounced it up to the wall and then we had to catch it before it touched the ground again.

All the tall people had the advantage. They would take it right out of my sights, and then yell out, "snags!" That was universal for "*I just took that.*" We never got tired of creating games. We had two squares with a basketball, truth or dare and etc. Whenever it was time for someone to go home, their mother would just step out of the house with their house robe on and yell, "Let's go, its dinnertime". Every time without fail, the only question was, "how long are you going to be gone?" The bottom line is that we had options, where nowadays, the communities are so bad that a single mother can't even trust a young man to carry her groceries to her car, let alone her house. It's just not safe or wise these days.

I ride through neighborhoods and the parks are void of swings, sliding boards, and etc. kids have no options other that to stand on the corner, join gangs, fight and sell drugs. It's our responsibility to give them some type of alternatives. We need to clean up our parks, pick up the trash, and empty beer cans. We can then give sports back to our children, take the drugs and violence off our blocks and give our daughters a chance to be prosperous. Give them their jump ropes back.

We have to reunite through interdependence in order to build our families back up to status quo. We have to bring family reunions back to a state of prevalence. Family reunions give us an opportunity to bond and to share valuable information that can be used in our quest to be successful. It's networking with a greater cause and a significant output. It builds a foundation for the younger generation to stand on. I remember getting in trouble when I was younger on the streets of Chicago and before the day was over, word of it would have traveled all the way to O'Hare Airport and then down to Memphis. Although it could've easily been perceived as gossip, when I got older, I understood that they were teaching me accountability. They wanted me to do well and if they could use this method as a deterrent, then they would. Whatever it took to keep me on the straight and narrow, aunties and uncles, etc, everybody participated in trying to shape my life properly and I can't find the words to express how grateful I am. I needed that shadow looming over my shoulder. I needed that push; this book would've been impossible without it.

Our neighbors were involved. They had the green light when it came to disciplining the children in the community. We had eyes on us wherever we went and I truly believe that I turned out to be a better person because of it.

I can hear Mr. and Mrs. Price right now asking me, "how am I doing, are you staying out of trouble"? I always responded with, "yes, no, ma'am or sir." For the rest of the day, when small signs of negativity would show up, I could hear those same voices repeating themselves in my head. To Mr. and Mrs. Price, Mrs. Duncan (who always made me peanut butter and jelly sandwiches), Mr. Herb who always said, "y'all stay off my grass," and to Mr. McGee, who always gave me a story. I thank you all for believing in me before I even knew how to believe in myself. There were several more adults keeping me grounded, I can go on and on with that list.

Joseph Joubert (175-1824 Pen see's no.261) once said that children have more need of models than of critics. The Talmud says that a child tells in the street what there father and mother say at home. A child knows nothing, no awareness of what is accepted and what is not. Any characteristic that a child obtains comes from others. Jacula Prudentum said, one father is more than a hundred school masters and I say that to give away your privilege to raise the children that you're blessed with, is to not know what a blessing is.

We don't have to succumb to the negativity that has been strategically placed in our neighborhoods. Liquor stores, currency exchanges, fast food restaurants, business's owned by other ethnic groups, we can overcome all of this. Over half of marriages end in divorce and more than two/thirds of second marriages, and that's because most people don't have a successful marriage to point to for reference. We've never had the opportunity to see a successful one up close and personal. As a kid, sometimes I use to wonder if it's even possible. When we experience difficulty in the relationship it's nothing for us to end it, because we haven't been taught the value of a marriage bond made before the eyes of God. It's a sacred bond that should be honored to your dying day and beyond. That's how we lost our commitment, trust, and dedication for each other. It was because of broken households. *When slavery started the first thing that ever happened was the separation of family, don't voluntarily separate your families now.* Cicero once said, "The first bond of society is marriage and the next, our children, then the whole family and all things in common. I conquer!

Chapter 10

Hip-Hop

(The positive and negative aspects of it)

It was unlike anything that I'd ever heard before the day I turned the radio on and heard "these are the brakes" by Curtis Blow, instantaneously it hypnotized me and took a hold of my soul. I was starving for more, because it seemed as if he was speaking directly to me. It's kind of like the way you'd feel after attending church for the first time in awhile. Every statement that the pastor makes seems as if it was especially spoken for you. I thought to myself, who is this, where is he from, and how did he make and record this type of music. I had questions and they begged for answers. I had no idea that this "new thing" would become such a big part of my life.

Around 1979 and the early 80's, blacks were still very entrenched within the battle of fighting for our social equality, just as we are today. Only at these times, others were less inclined to hear our complaints because we were not unified and we didn't have a voice. Our vote didn't count. Not even twenty years removed from the devastating assassinations of *Dr. Martin Luther King Jr. and Malcolm X,* there I was, a young brother (only turning 10 in 1982) completely oblivious to the world that I was living in.

There was no doubt in my mind that hip-hop was real and here to stay. I can't say that I knew it would blow like this, but I knew that it would be around in some capacity. "These are the brakes" performed by Curtis Blow, stood by itself for a while. Also, by me being from Chicago, we had our own form of expression called "house music" which came on 102.7 W.B.M.X. All of the time we had what you called hot mixes with producers and dj's such as Julian "Jumpin" Perez, Ron hardy, Pharris and others. There were always new tracks to be craved. Jack my body, French kiss, and love can't turn around. My hometown music will always be my first love and deeply a part of me. It was just something about this new form of music called hip-hop so I continued to study it. I searched for more of it every single day at the record shops, but I had no luck. I tried word of mouth, but no one could give me anything. Then one day I was going up and down the F.M. radio dial, and stumbled up on more hip-hop music. I'll never forget it. I immediately mastered the personality and the station. It was Pink house (R.I.P) who, would grow to be legendary, on 89.3 W.K.K.C

All I could think was, "eureka" because I had found it. I heard artists like Whodini, U.T.F.O (with my girl Roxanne Shante) and others. These were more than just songs to me, they stood for the possibilities of what I could achieve. I had very few living role models to follow. I didn't even have an idea of what it was I wanted to do with my life. That is until my boy Etienne gave me this tape that he dubbed from KKC called, "check out my melody." I called in to the radio station without permission, on punishment, just to find out what the artist name was. Still to this day, **Rakim** will always be my idle. His lyrical wordplay had far surpassed anything that was in rotation up to that point. Songs like, "these are the brakes" had real life lyrics accompanied with catchy choruses. The verses were conscious and very much so needed for those days and times. As a matter of fact those lyrics are still needed today, that's just how relevant they were. They were real easy to memorize, sing along to, and breakdown and dissect. Rakim came through the door and changed all of that, he had brought lyrical skills to the forefront, and clearly demonstrated what a microphone controller (m.c.) was. He unfolded deep concepts and showed that there was an art to m.c.ing and rhyming. That it wasn't just words thrown together, that just happened to rhyme, these were well thought out strategically placed words put together with a purpose. As *Chuck D* of the critically acclaimed group Public Enemy would later say, *"I don't rhyme for the sake of riddling."* I felt him too. Rakim was smooth, eloquent poetry, combined with wisdom and knowledge of self. Rakim's lyrics were so shrewd and profound that me and my friends couldn't listen to a song all the way through without looking at each other like, "what did he just say...noll..... I know that he didn't just say that." Take for example the first single I ever heard from him, as soon as check out my melody started you became engulfed in his wisdom and wordplay. *"Turn up the bass, check out my melody acknowledge the god, I'm letting knowledge be born and my name's the r a k I m not like the rest of them I'm not on a list. That's what I'm saying I got rhymes like a scientist!"* I had never heard anything like it in my whole life and that was in 1986, clearly making him ahead of his times. He was doing arithmetic on wax like it was nothing. "I'll take 7 m.c's put em' in a line and add 7 more brothers that think they can rhyme, well it'll take 7 more before I go for mine, now that's 21 m.c's ate up at the same time!" That was mc'ing at it's finest, ask another mc and he'll tell you the same. My man was quite nice and he was honing his craft and setting the precedent of how a microphone should be controlled.

He was the ultimate pioneer in my opinion, because he showed and represented the possibilities of where hip-hop could go. I learned of Islam for the first time through Rakim, he rhymed with a purpose *"so I'mma let my knowledge be born to a perfection all praises due to Allah and that's a blessing, add knowledge of self there's nothing I can't solve at 360" degrees I revolve it's an absolute fact it's not an act it's been proven indeed as I proceed to make the crowd keep moving"!* Classic lyrics from his single "move the crowd." After hearing the paid in full album I had told myself that if an individual can't flow like this, then I couldn't mess with it. I made up my mind a long time ago that if I was going to spend my allowance on a tape, if I was going to spend my hustling money on a song, then it had to be something that had substance, something that was tangible, something that I couldn't do myself. I needed lyrical conceptions and not some rinky dink play school rhymes that a third grader can make, and believe me when I tell you that that wasn't a shot at third graders either. I demanded skills for my dollar and Rakim met the criteria and then some. You'd be hard pressed to find a mc or a rapper from the 80's or 90's that wasn't influenced by the god mc, the 18th letter.

He spit bars with precision, in a way that was never showcased before. The lingo he brought to the forefront even goes unnoticed or blatantly stolen these days as If they didn't hear him the first time. On paid in full, he was the first artist that you ever heard refer to money as *dead presidents*, *"so I start my mission leave my residence, thinking how can I get some DEAD PRESIDENTS!"* He was the first to ever compare his flow to that of the Nile River. Never mind the fact that it's a dope simile, but it actually made me conscious to the fact that the Nile was indeed a river in Africa. His bars were trendsetters; he was versatile, and just raw, as I will demonstrate right now. Take for instance "microphone fiend" where his word play was off the charts, he said, *"ladies and gentlemen you're about to see, a past time hobby about to be taken to the maximum I can't relax see I'm hype as a hypochondriac cause the rap be one helluva antidote something can't smoke more than dope you tried to move away but you can't you broke more than cracked you should've backed up for those that act up need to be more than smacked up."* Before those bars, no one had even heard anyone double up on a word just to rhyme to other words. It was unconventional and brand new; plenty of artists do it with great success! Mc's like Jadakiss, Beanie Seigal, Fabulous, the late great Big L and a multitude of others, give great respect to this man; cause it would be difficult to find someone that wouldn't.

He said, "ladies and gentlemen you're about to see, a past time hobby about to be, taking to the *maximum* (which lyrically ended his 3rd bar, so focus in on the world maximum.) I can't relax see I'm hype as a hypochondriac because the rap is one." Not only did Rakim take the time to rhyme every syllable in the word maximum with the words *"rap be one."* But, in between the two words is where his work habits lay. This is where his love of poetry shined as he took the word relax and rhymed it with it's polar opposite hypochondriac. And just to reinforce the fact that he was conscious about his chose of words, he uttered that he was as hype as a hypochondriac, an "in between" and unappreciated rhyme pattern utilized by Rakim.

Such as In mahogany when he subtly placed, intervene and interrupt in between "rush" and "up." Once again, by using two compound words that started with "inter" he showed his love for the art. Please believe me when I tell you that every up and coming artist peeped that. Rakim even knew it as displayed inside the legendary joint "I ain't no joke" when he said *"cause you'll get fried in the end when you pretend to be, competing cause I can put your mind on pause, and I'm complete when you compare my rhyme with yours, I wake you up and as I stair in your face you seem stunned, remember me the one you got your idea from."* He was a lyrical genius and he's definitely the reason I wanted to m.c. Plenty of artists have paid homage Buckshot of Black moon, re-rapped I ain't no joke, corrupt said "Rakim never joked so why should I loc. Now that's my idle" 2 Pac utilized Rakim's bars from Eric B for president when he said "bare witness to the dopest damn rhyme I wrote taking off my coat clearing my throat." Even 50 said that my favorite rapper use to sing, "check, check out my melody." Even in one of my earlier rhymes I said *"I remember when I first started it my man ace gave me a tape with Rakim on a part of it, up in my crib all it did was sit but something kept telling me to bump it a bit and once I popped it in couldn't believe it and until this day "check out my melody" is still the shit".* With total respect to afrikabambata and every pioneer that had skills, Rakim was the personification of what an m.c. is to me.

I love hip hop, I love poetry and therefore I would be remised if I didn't acknowledge the true pioneers such as *Gwendolyn Brooks (whom is my role model), Toni Morrison, Langston Hughes, Nikki Giovanni, Alice Walker, Phyllis Wheatley and many more.* And when it comes to music, the godfather of soul James Brown, R.I.P. stands alone.

The list of lovely mc's to bless the mic are countless in number but K.R.S one as well as Chuck D stand out in my era. They always had a message that lasted longer than the song, as a matter of fact, the knowledge they gave me in the 80's is still with me today, Chuck D attacked relevant issued and forced me to become politically conscious, they gave me the strength needed to pump my first and say fight the power. KRS one did the same for me. It was all about edutainment. I stopped eating pork because of KRS one. I learned that cocaine business controlled America. It meant that the hood didn't have the means to create the drug, so it had to come from somewhere else, and that "somewhere else" was how those in power continue to stay in power and run this country. "We fight inflation yet the presidents still on vacation." These were things that the public school system were failing to teach me hip hop didn't necessarily raise me, but it taught me things that I still haven't learned in any other place and time, so call it what you may.

Those in other music genres tended to believe that this new form of music was a fad. They said that it wouldn't last to see 25yrs, but hip-hop is still here alive and well. Through the b-boys, crazy legs, and the rock steady crew. Through the taggers, through the mc crews such as biz markie, Dougie Fresh, Slick Rick, LL cool J, Run DMC, Ghetto Boys, N.W.A, big Daddy Kane, Gang Starr, Nas, and Wu-Tang. Mc lyte, Amg, Boss, Mc Breed, Death Row records, Dre, Snoop, rage, Rbx, Corrupt, Daz, Foxxy Brown, 2 Pac, Biggie, Outkast, U.G.K, ludacris, 2 live crew, ice cube, scarface, X-clan, Onyx, U.T.F.O, Salt-n-Pepa, Common sense, Jay z, kanye, Twista, Crucial conflict, Do or die, Da brat, T.I., Jadakiss(d-block), the list can go on for ever. The point is that we're still here standing stronger than ever.

Don't get me wrong though because there's a boatload of things that need to be corrected. Somehow, someway, we've lost our direction. For some reason we've been brain washed to think that the struggle is over, when it's really just beginning. We don't need a Don Imus or other sorts to make us conscious of ourselves, it shouldn't take that, but there are no strange happenings, law governs all events and everything happens for a reason. It's **been** time for us to recognize our power and influence. See when hip-hop started it was our only outlet to vent, so we did it in whatever fashion we felt suitable. It was built up pain that made us say "fuck the police" and write songs like "cop killer" it was necessary to get our point across. Nigga, bitch, and hoe served its purpose in that era, even if it was to show us where we were slipping. I was bumping it all day, everyday, I still do, but today I'm just a little bit more conscious of what I'm listening to. As an artist one has to understand that we're not underground anymore, on the contrary, we're the number one music genre in the world. Within that comes responsibility and knowledge of the fact that the world is listening when you use bitch, hoe or nigga in a lyric. So when you're on stage performing to a predominantly white audience, expect them to recite your lyrics word for word.

It puts everybody in an awkward position because these young people, not of African decent are true genuine fans of hip hop, just as Latino's and blacks and once we (they) spend their money to purchase a c.d. the last thing an individual wants to do is have to comb through the songs to find out which lyrics are acceptable for me to use and which ones are not. It's up to the artist to understand that he is universal and setting the precedent for the rest of the world to follow.

To my sisters, I know that there's been a lot said about the exploitation of black women in videos. I understand that it depicts all or the majority of black women in that manner and that the words bitch and hoe used by your own black men make it that much worse. You have young boys walking around using these words randomly on sisters like its cool. It's deplorable, but at some point and time action has to come in and override conversation, so what I'm saying is that sisters can't sit and wait for everybody else to get it right, when has that ever worked in history! No, sisters have to take a stand and start telling everyone else, including black men, what's acceptable and what's not! Mothers, you need to start raising your daughters with a stronger since of urgency, because if you don't raise her then the streets will. Mothers need to be involved in healthy relationships or at least prosperous situations so that the daughter may see first hand how a man should treat a woman when he loves her. Please, please, please teach your daughter that her body is a temple, because it is. She is to be taught that sex is something that is shared with another to consummate love, not something that's given away like government cheese. It's our job to teach our little girls what their worth is. Once this happens, fewer and fewer females will be willing to take off all of their clothes just to have camera time in a rapper's video.

We'll have fewer females that believe that love is expressed in the form of physical abuse. Teenage pregnancy levels would drop, the transportation of diseases would reduce, and our daughters will instantaneously be given a higher chance at succeeding in what it is they aspire for. It's not hip-hop's responsibility to raise our children, but in saying that, I do feel as though it's hip-hop's responsibility not to misguide our youth. Once more, you are sadly mistaken and misinformed if you believe that hip hop as a whole will screen itself and do the right thing for your sake, that's your responsibility. There is no prerequisite to be a rapper; a high school diploma isn't necessary, although education does uplift every aspect of your life. All you have to be is focused, business oriented, and determined.

I'm definitely not criticizing hip hop though, I rap myself, and I'm just saying that it's naïve for us to believe that every rapper has a high level of morals and value. Many could care less about who their music affects; nobody is holding them accountable. It has become all about the dollar, only a few still respect the craft. There's a mad dash for the financial gain that can come from hip hop and people are coming for it by any means necessary and I can't say that I blame them. I or no one else can knock a person trying to better their position in life, the only question I have is, at what cost?

Hip Hop is universal now and it's synonymous with everything, everywhere. Everyone has stuck their claws into Hip Hop, raping it for whatever they can. They could care less about the preservation of it, all they care about is the finances that can be made off of it, and the detrimental part of this is that some of our most prominent rappers think the same way. It's deeply embedded in sports, fast food commercials, soft drinks, and car dealerships. Just listen to all these commercials that subtly play hip-hop in the background. Next, they place a face that looks like yours in the commercial to further subtly market it to you. It would be easier for me to make a list of the things that weren't influenced. The small amount they pay the artist to promote the product is crumbs compared to what they make in profit. I'm not mad at the athlete at all because he has to feed his family just like I have to feed mine, the bigger picture though, is that our culture, genre, and creativeness are being stolen right before our eyes. First it was the pyramids, and now, you get the point.

Why should those who can't rap continue to make the most money within our music? We have to start being more business oriented. Some of us, we market products of these companies for free. When are we going to start recognizing our power? Even more, once we fully grasp the concept that it's not the material things that makes us hot, the better suited we are to embrace our own individual talents.

I don't need to pay $200 for a pair of Jordan's to validate my skill level on the court. I don't have to work on swag; my skill set is my swag. I don't have to own a platinum chain to validate my status. These things are cool to have, but it's the mentality behind it that matters. Silver, gold, and platinum didn't have a value or price until we gave it on. That's why these hip-hop summits with *Ben Chavez, Russell Simmons*, and others are so important, because they stress economics, moral obligations, and unity.

I think that a union should be formed to where as; every rapper in it must partake and find ways to help our youth progress. It would serve all sorts of purposes, it would hold everyone accountable for their actions, information of business ventures could be exchanged and perhaps medical, dental, and death funds could be discussed. Rappers don't think about healthcare or 401k plans when they sign on the dotted line. Throughout the images that are given on our videos, new comers are led to believe that they will immediately become millionaires making money hand over fist, but that's simply just not the case.

Most of the cars you see in videos, the jewelry, along with the glamorous woman are rented for services. Jay z said it best when he wrote, "mc's got now and later rhymes, they rap about it now and hope to get it later." The mandatory meeting, once or twice a year, would do justice for us all around the board.

I commend people like *Michael Eric Dyson, cousin Jeff,* (from B.E.T) etc. for the powerful roles they play in trying to consciously uplift the hip hop community and our people as a whole. I love B.E.T, and I can't wait until we start airing cartoons for the kids in the morning, and educational programs after school. It's all about uplifting our youth, the videos are entertaining, but we need more learning programs, from all sources. We say that black history month is really an everyday celebration, but where is the evidence of it? Where are the after School programs that continue to educate once the regular school day is complete? Study history. Read as often as you can. Where are the mentors that come into the schools and motivate our youth to be great? Where are the programs that teach us about our history, where is the toll free hotline number that helps our youth with their homework? We can't continue to sit back and wait for other people to teach us about us, that hasn't happened in four hundred years, we have to teach our kids about *Phyllis Wheatley, Nat turner, Eldridge Cleavor; etc.*

Hip Hop belongs to us, we gave birth to it and in order for it to sustain life, we have to nurture it properly. We are being viewed by the whole world everyday and it's up to every one of us to make sure that the picture is a positive and profound one. In the mean time let's continue to give hope back to our children.

Thank you for allowing me to express myself. Thank you for giving critical thought to this book, and electing not to just rush through it. This is my legacy. The one that will be left for my kids to reflect back on when they need a reminder on who their father was, and I want them to be proud. I want them to understand that any person that tries to limit you is not your friend. So to my offspring (my bloodline) Essence, Diamonte, and Shereena, I need you'll to know that daddy loves you more than I love myself. I know that it sounds cliché, but if I had to leave you with words of advice it would simply be GO HARD!!!!!!!

Words From The Author

Although words can't truly describe my feeling, I would like to thank you all from the bottom of my heart for supporting me in my dream of becoming more today than I was yesterday. The time I spent incarcerated was extremely trying, stressful on so many different levels. There wasn't a day that passed that I didn't think of my children and with each birthday that passed, I felt them slipping further and further away from me. Sometimes it was hard to sleep at night, I wouldn't wish that on my worst enemy. The damage that is done to the family is all most indelible. It still pains me to know that I missed my auntie C.C. and grandma Cooke's funerals, I can't get that back and it hurts like hell, the jail said that they didn't consider that immediate family. My grandmother raised me, but let's move on. That's why this book means so much to me; it's my way of proving to **ME** that I am somebody, somebody capable of doing great things in the time that Allah (PBUH) hath given me on these plains of things made manifest. It's important to me because I want my children to know that no matter the circumstances, they can achieve anything that their hearts desire, because their father is living proof of it. I need them to know that the greatest heights are always achieved by those who have been to the greatest depths. When you're life is over how will you be remembered? What will be the impression that you make on the world? **I can't wait to be at your book signing, or whatever great thing that you decide to do. Always remember though, Go Hard!!**
Please feel free to voice your opinion to the author at dkcooke@att.net

"If We Must Die" by Claude McKay

If we must die, let it not be like hogs
Hunted and penned in an inglorious spot
While round us bark the mad and hungry dogs
Making their mock at our accursed lot.

If we must die, O let us nobly die
So that our precious blood may not be shed in vain
Then even the monsters we defy
Shall be constrained to honor us though dead

O kinsmen! We must meet the common foe!
Though far outnumbered, let us show us brave,
And for their thousand blows, deal one deathblow!
What though before us lies that open grave

Like men we'll face the murderous, cowardly pack,
Pressed to the wall, dying, but fighting back!